Battenberg Britain

Battenberg Britain

A nostalgic tribute to the
foods we loved

Nigel Cassidy and Philippa Lamb

MICHAEL O'MARA BOOKS

First published in Great Britain in 2009 by
Michael O'Mara Books Limited
9 Lion Yard
Tremadoc Road
London SW4 7NQ

A CIP catalogue record for this book is available from the British Library.

Papers used by Michael O'Mara Books Limited are natural, recyclable products made from wood grown in sustainable forests. The manufacturing processes conform to the environmental regulations of the country of origin.

ISBN: 978-1-84317-378-6

1 2 3 4 5 6 7 8 9 10

www.mombooks.com

Cover design by Design 23
Designed and typeset by Design 23

Printed and bound in Italy by L.E.G.O.

ACKNOWLEDGMENTS

The authors would like to apologize to Ann, Ruth, Claire and Felix, for force-feeding them faggots, fish paste and Vesta curries in the interests of research. Our gratitude also to our courageous tasting panel of Michelle Bark, Helena Bohoslawec, Aileen Jackson, Chris K. Jones, Sue Keefe, Phil and Helen Lowe, Jane Mawer, Eddie Menday, and Francis and Jo Pearce. Thanks for all your delicious food memories – and for not eating all the Tunnock's Teacakes.

PICTURE ACKNOWLEDGEMENTS

Pages 1, 6, 7, 9, 12, 19, 23, 30, 44, 64, 68, 89, 95, 113, 122: special photography by Chris K. Jones
Page 73: Alamy
Pages 11, 15, 35, 48, 51, 66, 82, 92, 98/99, 107: The Advertising Archives
Pages 37, 46, 62, 70, 79, 85, 88, 91: Hwa Young Jung
Page 87: Mary Evans Picture Library
Page 49, 78: by kind courtesy of www.historyworld.co.uk
Page 97: by kind courtesy of www.JonWilliamson.com
Every effort has been made to trace the copyright holders of the images in this book. Any errors or omissions that may have occurred are inadvertent, and anyone with any copyright queries is invited to write to the publishers, so that a full acknowledgement may be included in subsequent editions of the work.

CONTENTS

INTRODUCTION

It's probably over-egging it to say that we live to eat, but there's no denying we both adore food. It's the infinite variety that's got us hooked – the endless possibilities of a culinary world embracing everything from haute cuisine to SPAM. What could be more enjoyable than tasting a dish you've never ordered before or inviting friends round as unwitting guinea pigs in some outlandish culinary experiment? Well, quite a lot of things obviously, but this is a book for all the family.

Like all good foodies, our supermarket trolleys overflow with exotic vegetables, organic meats, artisan breads and Marmite. Marmite? Yes, Marmite. And fish fingers and Worcestershire Sauce and, of course, Battenberg cake. Because no matter how virtuous we've become about home cooking and healthy eating, there are still certain tins and packets we can't do without. They're the affordable, easy-to-prepare foods we grew up with in the 1960s and 1970s, from the alchemy in a bowl that is Angel Delight to the prosaic pleasure of a corned beef and piccalilli sandwich;

the comforting foods of our childhood that millions like us mysteriously find themselves missing like mad the moment we set foot outside the country.

One man's meat is another woman's poison and we have to admit to the odd disagreement about the merits of one or two of these products, but what intrigues us both are the colourful and often bizarre histories behind these famous names: the long-lost tales of the mustard, custard and syrup barons who made them possible and the clever advertising that kept us buying. Who could resist finding out more about the eccentric inventor of HP Sauce – a man who wanted to use zebras to haul his promotional carts round the country? Or the poignant death of the military hero on the Camp Coffee label? And what about the unlikely suggestion that

Messrs Tate and Lyle never actually came face to face? They're the fascinating stories that today's brand managers may never have heard – or would sometimes rather forget.

So forget about fusion food and tuck in to a nostalgic British feast instead. It's your family history – on a plate.

FRAY BENTOS TINNED PIES

If you truly want to dine like its 1969, then a pie cooked in its very own tin would be the perfect choice for your main course. But that doesn't mean those famous steak or chicken pies are now culinary museum pieces. Canned pie sales at Fray Bentos alone are worth over £20 million a year.

Problem numero uno is wrestling the lid off. The lip is deep, and the circumference of the can is 48 cm. Most of us deploy a tin opener so rarely these days it's usually a rubbish one, and many people end up using brute force and pliers – always a dangerous combination. It's probably why the makers have been known to soothe people who complain with the gift of a tin opener.

The best bit …

Once the lid is off, first impressions are uninspiring – all you can see is that wet, lardy-looking layer of raw pastry covering the pre-cooked contents. However, stick the tin in the oven and you will be rewarded by a magnificent, though curiously always lopsided, puffed pastry crust – with that strata of soft, yummy, gravy-soaked stuff underneath … and that's before you get to the tender, if very slightly metallic meat and gravy. If you don't like the soggy pastry layer, just turn over the whole crust during the cooking time. But why wouldn't you? It's the best bit.

During the 25–30 minutes' cooking time, you could copy the serving suggestions on the lid and prepare a simple medley of *al dente* broccoli and baby carrots. Or, as is more likely with today's pie-lovers, put on some oven chips and read *Viz* magazine until it's done. Oh, and if you forget to check the instructions before getting the lid off, well now you're stuffed, because they're printed on the bottom. And don't even think about cooking your pie without removing the lid (or slipping it in

Survivability	*6/10*
Trolley Embarrassment Factor	*9/10*
Versatility	*LOW*

the microwave), unless you want to replace your entire kitchen.

Fray Bentos pies may be resolutely British, but until 1958 they were made in Uruguay in what was said to be the largest food factory in the free world. The company was already renowned for its corned beef and had done sterling work feeding vast numbers of allied troops in the Second World War.

Celebrity nosh

Tinned pies also have a top celebrity fan – heart throb actor Sean Bean. He has tins shipped to his film locations, where he douses them in Henderson's Relish, a delicacy from his home town of Sheffield. Another surprising enthusiast is chef and foodie writer Simon Hopkinson – journalist Lynne Barber spotted the familiar tin in his kitchen.

Over the last fifty years, Fray Bentos must have played some part in the sad decline of home pie-making. Yet hopefully most of us aren't as snooty as a woman on Jamie Oliver's website whose mother told her that Fray Bentos tins were ideal for making homemade Yorkshire pudding. So she bought the pies, threw away the contents and re-used the tins. Silly moo.

AMBROSIA CREAMED RICE

No one could accuse Alfred Morris of modesty when he built a new creamery and named it Ambrosia after the food said to have made the Greek Gods immortal. Actually, the Greek allusion was a bit rubbish because it was the Romans who first made a kind of rice pudding as a cure for seasickness. And anyway, Mr Morris's first Ambrosial product back in 1917 wasn't rice pudding – it was powdered milk.

At the time, Britain was far from the pastoral nirvana shown on the tins. The First World War hadn't ended and there were food shortages and rationing. Alfred's big idea was to use rollers to dry surplus milk from the lush dairy farms around his home at Lifton in Devon to make a rich baby food. But his biggest brainwave was in the 1930s, when he started to can cooked rice pudding. The new pud went down a storm with the Forces; word spread and the company daringly branched out into macaroni and tapioca (though the less said about those sticky frogspawn-like globules the better).

Jam or nutmeg?

Fans of proper, oven-cooked rice pudding with brown skin can never be bought off with the tinned variety. Yet Ambrosia does get close – the soft rice slips down in a warm creamy wave with only a hint of tin somewhere in the aftertaste. That rather strange shade of beige remains a bit of a puzzle but maybe it's to do with the milk caramelizing. Mind you, that's nothing to the colour it turns after Nigel has stirred in his requisite dessertspoonful of raspberry jam. Needless to say, Philippa

Survivability	*4/10*
Trolley Embarrassment Factor	*9/10*
Versatility	*LOW*

nows how they make it so creamy.

prefers a light dusting of freshly ground organic Indonesian nutmeg. There's posh for you. It's only out of a tin, love.

Ambrosia is famous for its charmingly stereotypical TV advertising, although a recent campaign featuring a Devon farmer astride a cow attracted a bizarre complaint from an RSPCA official who thought it might encourage people to approach cows in fields and try to ride them. The original adverts featured the voice of Pete Budd, lead singer of the chart-topping spoof folkies the Wurzels, who intoned that immortal line 'Devon knows 'ow they make it so creamy'. Don't tell anyone, but Pete was actually born in Somerset.

ARCTIC ROLL

The Arctic Roll has always inspired deep affection and remains in pole position in the frozen desserts pantheon. This is remarkable – we are, after all, just talking about sponge stuck to a log of plain vanilla ice cream with a smear of jam. Not an obvious pud to get the taste buds tingling, even in the 1970s, yet in many households it was all but piped into the dining room. It was what you had if it was someone's birthday, you'd passed an exam, or Mum just felt like giving everyone a treat. As consumers, we were learning that those extra special moments could be bought at a price at the local supermarket and even today good old Arctic Roll is being unearthed from the deep freeze all over again. Both Birds Eye and Lyons Maid are playing the nostalgia card and have relaunched their own versions as recession-beating treats.

The mysteries of physics

So what's so great about it? Well, for us it's that

combination in your mouth of the ice-cold smoothness of the ice cream, cut through by the contrasting texture of the sweet damp sponge. We always thought that the fact that the sponge never comes out of the pack frozen was one of the great unsolved mysteries of physics. However, when we asked the boffins at Birds Eye, they explained it's because much of the water content is driven off during the baking process, so there's not enough left to form ice.

What is surprising is how many people insist on eating up the sponge first on its own, even though it tastes very much like the padding in a Jiffy bag. Apparently, they do this to avoid putting the different constituent parts in the mouth simultaneously — an approach to eating which to our minds suggests an urgent need for therapy.

Birds Eye didn't invent Arctic Roll. It inherited it in 1959, when it bought out an independent ice cream and frozen foods factory in Eastbourne, on the Sussex coast. That company belonged to a Dr Ernest Velden, a Czech lawyer who took British citizenship. He died in 1990 — and there the trail goes cold, so to speak. Dr Velden was almost certainly the inventor, but whether he was emulating some fancy continental or even American ice-cream cake he had enjoyed somewhere on his travels we'll never know.

Twenty-five miles a month!

Thirty years ago, Birds Eye were selling twenty-five miles of ice-cream roll every month, and it all went brilliantly until the early 1980s, when the arctic winds blew in its nemesis — Viennetta, all swirly ripples and crunchy chocolate bits. How could our old favourite compete? Despite a flurry of 'Save Our Arctic Roll' nonsense in the press, Birds Eye Walls eventually suspended production.

Unlike Viennetta, the Arctic Roll also failed to crack the export market. Go on — just go to a café in any town in the Arctic Circle and try ordering one. We can almost guarantee you'll get something with herring in it. They do have Icebox Cake in the US, but the filling is whipped cream. Mind you, what we call Swiss roll they call jelly roll, so let's not go there.

Survivability	*4/10*
Trolley Embarrassment Factor	*8/10*
Versatility	*LOW*

SMASH

If Smash had been advertised by some bossy 1970s housewife lecturing us on how yummy it was, we probably wouldn't think of it as fondly as we do now. What got those frankly unappetizing packets of instant dried potato mix flying off the shelves was the masterful 1974 TV ad from the Boase Massimi Pollitt agency. It's been hailed as the best TV character advertisement of all time, beating Captain Birdseye and Bertie Bassett into a cocked hat.

Who can forget those boggle-eyed Smash Martians, rolling around and laughing like drains as they watched us earthlings laboriously peeling potatoes, boiling them for twenty of our minutes and then smashing them to all to bits with our metal knives. We didn't even mind when they mocked us as 'clearly a most primitive people'.

Survivability	4/10
Trolley Embarrassment Factor	10/10
Versatility	MEDIUM

What could be easier?

The agency ad team must have known from their brief that while Smash produced a bowlful of passable mash, few people preferred it to real potatoes. So the ad cleverly made no claims whatsoever about what it tasted like. The message from our metallic friends was simply that Smash was a high-tech, fuss-free alternative to proper spuds. What could be easier than pouring the granules into a bowl and adding boiling water?

Instant mashed potato flakes were invented in 1962 by a Canadian called Edward A. Asselbergs who worked for the Agriculture Department in Ottawa. The technique he developed was used to create lightweight field rations that could be reconstituted by campers or the military.

Smash was originally Cadbury's Smash. The chocolate company had decided to diversify, and its first non-chocolate product had been Marvel, a powdered milk. This set the company down the road of 'instant' as being the next big thing. A Cadbury's team came across the technology that would be used for Smash in America, signed up the rights and never looked back. Cadbury Nigeria even launched Pound-o-Yam, which was, you guessed it, instant yams. However, Cadbury's eventually decided to sell off Smash, which is now part of the Premier Foods empire.

Forty years later, Smash remains a good seller and enough is produced to make up 140 million servings every year. As for those chortling visitors from the Red Planet, well even they keep making comebacks and have become quite an extended family, with Martian pets and a range of games, and other extraterrestrial merchandise.

Even the French do it

As for those gourmands across the Channel, even the French, aren't averse to a bit of cheating with their spuds. They have an inexplicable weakness for a powdered potato product called Mousseline, which turns out slightly sloppy, which is just how they seem to like it.

We decided to make a retro-supper of Bangers and Smash. For a start, we were surprised to discover on opening the packet, that Smash is now powder rather than granules, though it still smells like ready-salted crisps. Made up, it's certainly creamy and looks the part, in fact it's probably better than it used to be. But it still just can't quite capture the exquisite taste and texture of the real thing. Were we really so idle thirty years ago that we preferred eating this stuff to wielding a potato-peeler? Maybe revisiting your culinary past is like sleeping with an 'ex'. Try it again for old times' sake, by all means, but you probably won't want seconds. Some things are best enjoyed in the memory.

DEL MONTE TINNED PINEAPPLE

How are the mighty fallen. Back in the seventeenth century, a single pineapple would have set you back the price of a small car in today's money. The ultimate luxury food, Charles II even had his portrait painted with one, just to remind everyone how wealthy he really was. Leap forward to 1901, and the glory days came to an abrupt end: tinned pineapple went on sale for the first time and suddenly anyone could eat like a king.

Upside-down cake anyone?

As every schoolgirl knows, the world has Christopher Columbus to thank for the pineapple. He 'discovered' them on the Caribbean island of Guadeloupe in 1493, unimaginatively christened them 'pina' because they looked like pine cones, and took some back to Spain. Highly perishable and tricky to grow outside their natural environment, pineapples remained a rarity until 1911, when an engineer named Henry Ginaca revolutionized the canned fruit industry by inventing a machine which could shell, core, top and tail one hundred of them in under a minute. Mass-market pineapples had arrived and having finally got their hands on them, the hoi polloi were quick to invent creative ways to use them. In 1925, when the Hawaiian Pineapple Company asked housewives to send in their favourite recipes, they were showered with 2,500 versions of upside-down cake alone.

The Del Monte company started canning pineapple in the early years of the 1900s, having made a first foray into food supplying coffee to the ritzy Hotel Del Monte in Monterey. The famous red shield label made its first appearance in 1909 and seven years later the company joined what was to become an immensely powerful alliance of fellow Californian fruit growers known as Calpak. Years before the famous 'The man from Del Monte – he say "yes"!' TV campaign, the company marketed its fruit on quality rather than price. As far back as 1920 the bold assurance 'not a label but a guarantee' appeared on the tins. In an era when canning was still a far from perfect science, the strategy was a smart one and the brand survived the depression years and the Second World War bcforo blossoming into a global player in the 1960s. Because the tinned variety was packed in syrup, it was sweeter and more reliable than fresh pineapples, which had to be shipped to Europe unripe, where most shoppers wouldn't have had any idea how to tackle the prickly job of cutting one up.

Del Monte never looked back, although its ownership did change hands several times. Even now, it is divided between two separate outfits but the product is much the same as it always was. It's now available in rings, wedges, 'tidbits' or even crushed, for those who find slices too dentally demanding.

Survivability	*9/10*
Trolley Embarrassment Factor	*3/10*
Versatility	*HIGH*

Del Monte packed–at the ripe moment!

Every sunlit slice comes fresh from the can. As ripe and sweet as the day it left the plantation. Del Monte* Brand pineapples get every hour of sunshine they need to ripen to the moment when sweetness and tartness balance. Then they're packed on this very same day. That's the Del Monte secret. **Peel a can this lunchtime!**

Registered trade mark of the California Packing Corporation

A symbol of hospitality

Sadly, familiarity bred contempt for the pineapple in the late twentieth century when it began falling victim to some truly horrible culinary abuses (we're talking gammon, Fanny Craddock cocktail sticks and cubes of cheddar cheese), but this beautiful and mathematically perfect fruit can console itself with the many tributes paid to it by stonemasons the world over. Carved into buildings as diverse as pre-Incan ruins in South America, colonial mansions in the US and, perhaps most extraordinary of all, a colossal stone folly in Stirlingshire, the fruit has been immortalized as an international symbol of hospitality. Early colonists in the Americas took up the native Carib Indian tradition of hanging the fruit over their doors as a sign of welcome, and we have a former governor of Virginia to thank for the famous 'Stirlingshire Pineapple' landmark. Evidently not a man to hide his light under a bushel, the fourth Earl of Dunmore is said to have commissioned the eponymous folly topped with a seventy-five-foot stone pineapple to mark his return from the New World in 1777. What he had against change of address cards we shall never know.

HP SAUCE

HP Sauce might just as well show the impressive Madrid Parliament or the Knight's Hall in The Hague on the front of its famous red and blue label, instead of the familiar picture of the Houses of Parliament. In October 2006, forty-two MPs signed a Commons motion deploring that Parliament was still on the label – even though production had been moved out of the West Midlands to factories on the Continent.

Yes, 2006 was that fateful year when Heinz, based in Pittsburgh USA, halted an unbroken century of British tradition. It made the change soon after buying HP from the French food giant Danone. The Aston factory was demolished, and 125 jobs were lost. All that remains is the giant landmark HP Sauce sign, which was given to the Birmingham City Museum. This wasn't the first factory closure in the region, and it won't be the last. What rankled was the fact that the brand was still shamelessly trading on its British heritage. Only weeks before, HP had been campaigning to save local greasy spoons, suggesting Britain's cafés could go the same way as red phone boxes and London

Routemaster buses. There was talk of a nationwide boycott, but it came to nothing. As Heinz probably hoped, by now most people have forgotten about the row, or don't really mind where their HP is made, as long as it makes their bacon butties taste nice. So HP Sauce remains a top selling condiment, knocking out 27.5 million bottles a year.

The secret formula

HP is popular because it packs a punch. The secret formula includes spices, sweet molasses, dates and even tamarind, a fashionable ingredient with today's fusion chefs. For many, a fry-up at home or in a café would be unthinkable without it. Brown sauce was invented as a kind of bottled antidote to the remorselessly functional British diet. We never used to eat exotic food, and we still can't grow much of it in our climate. So instead we slathered our sausage and chips with concoctions brewed up in satanic mills from fancy ingredients gathered from over the Empire.

HP Sauce goes back to 1875, when Edwin Samson Moore, a Midlands vinegar baron, wanted to add a brand name sauce to

his repertoire. Moore was on a visit to a Nottingham grocer, F. G. Garton, when he smelt a delicious aroma brewing at the back of the shop. It was 'HP' sauce, so named because it was rumoured to have been seen on dining tables in the House of Commons. Garton owed Moore £150, but Moore was more than happy to cancel the debt in exchange for the recipe and the use of the name.

An overnight success

Moore took his time – HP wasn't launched until 1903. But it was close to an overnight success. The masses could cheer up their inferior cuts of meat and leftovers with a taste hitherto only enjoyed by the rich. Business also boomed thanks to poster campaigns and a fleet of promotional donkey carts. Moore had apparently wanted to use zebras, but was persuaded that they couldn't easily be trained.

You can perhaps see why Heinz felt justified in keeping Parliament on the label – it had always related to where the product was consumed, not where it was made. Famous fans today include Jamie Oliver (does he eat it secretly on Turkey Twizzlers?), Keith Richards and Tom Hanks. Frank Bruno doesn't

count – he was well paid to advertise it. More curiously, the late former British Prime Minister Sir Harold Wilson was said to be an HP enthusiast, a suggestion which did his cultivated 'man of the people' image no harm. But much later his wife Mary revealed the truth – he actually preferred the posher Lea and Perrins Worcestershire Sauce.

One curious footnote: for more than sixty years, a section of the HP Sauce bottle label was printed in French. It was just a quirky marketing ploy to get people talking – the truth is that the French wouldn't be seen dead pouring an English sauce on their fancy cuisine. Yet, in their defence, it has to be said that when a French firm owned HP Sauce, even they never dared to move the factory across the English Channel.

Survivability	*10/10*
Trolley Embarrassment Factor	*2/10*
Versatility	*LOW*

JACOB'S CREAM CRACKERS

Cream crackers are approximately seven cms square and contain about thirty-four calories each. Don't take our word for it because we just don't have time to go round taking the vital statistics of savoury biscuits, but there are people out there who do, and that's what they tell us. Now, thirty-four calories isn't much, but then again you have to factor in all the butter and cheese you load on top. Only people who are trying to beat the world record for eating three in the shortest possible time eat their crackers naked (49.15 seconds at the time of writing, in case you were wondering).

Don't let the name mislead you – there is no cream in cream crackers. United Biscuits, the company that owns the market-leading Jacob's brand, says the word 'cream' refers to the way the ingredients are 'creamed' together before being baked, and they should know because Jacob's have been making crackers since 1885. Not that they actually invented them: the story goes that William Jacob heard about the crackers sold out of barrels in American grocery stores and decided to have a go at making some in his Dublin factory. This was what's known in the trade as 'a very good idea', because they're still selling hand over fist today. These days, the Jacob's Company alone makes twenty different types of cracker. Yet it's somehow reassuring that this one, with its traditional orange label, outsells upstarts like Cheddars, Choice Grain and even Nigel's personal favourite, the celebrated Cornish Wafer.

Right in the cream crackers …

It's probably best to pass swiftly over the less savoury meaning that the phrase 'cream crackered' has come to signify in cockney rhyming slang. If you don't already know, we're not about to spell it out but male readers might like to ponder

Survivability	*10/10*
Trolley Embarrassment Factor	*0/10*
Versatility	*LOW*

possible endings to the sentence 'The football hit me right in the ...' More delightfully, the distinctive orange packet has been immortalized worldwide as the cracker of choice for Wallace of Wallace and Grommit fame. Wensleydale appears to be the cartoon inventor's favourite accompaniment, but he's not really fussed as long as there's some sort of cheese involved.

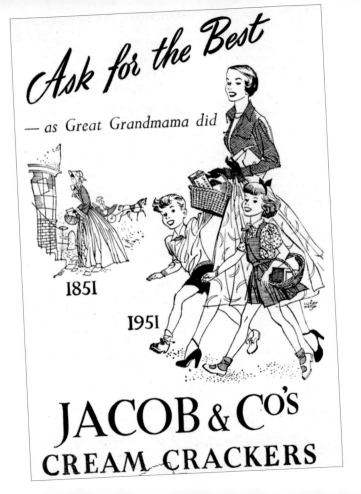

Back in the real world, a friend of ours claims that she has cream crackers to thank for her large family: apparently they were the only thing that cured her morning sickness and she swears she'd never have been able to face another pregnancy without them. And apparently the older you get, the more you seem to fancy them: as one older friend gamely admitted to us, 'If you've got funny teeth, you want things that snap easily.'

American in origin they may be, but in many ways the cream cracker is Britain distilled into a biscuit. A little bland, perhaps, but crisp and fulfilling, not too sweet or salty, gets along with everyone and is entirely reliable. It was recently suggested that handing out welcoming biscuits to arriving airline passengers might improve the vibe at the UK Border. For all the reasons above, we feel that it's the Jacob's Cream Cracker that should be selected for the task, ideally partnered with one of those impossible-to-open miniature packs of cheddar cheese. That would keep people occupied in the queues for hours on end.

CHEESE FOOTBALLS

Turkey and plum pudding might be the star turns on Christmas Day but it was always the edible bit players that made us feel truly Christmassy in the 60s and 70s. There were so many weird things that only appeared in the shops in December: net stockings stuffed with all our favourite chocolate bars; exotic-looking tins of bright green Turkish delight; Warninks Advocaat; Eat Me Dates, and, of course, Cheese Footballs.

An anaemic-looking wafer sphere crammed with a frankly odd-tasting cheese filling might not be everyone's first choice with their aperitifs on Christmas Day, but they're strangely irresistible when you're lying like a stranded whale in front of the Bond movie after lunch. As for their origins, no one we spoke to can recall seeing them much before the 1960s. They were always served at the kind of cocktail party where glasses full of cigarettes were put out for guests or handed round with the canapés.

Full time for festive favourite

Genuine Jacob's Cheese Footballs can be tricky to find. Trawl the consumer advice sites in the run-up to 25 December every year and the trickle of anxious inquiries soon becomes a flood. Regional shortages are common and swaps, bartering and outright bribery are by no means unknown. Recession or no recession, it's dog eat dog when it comes to the last drum in the shop and when word of a new delivery flashes round the net, no supermarket is safe from the ravening (well, 'ravening' may be a slight exaggeration, but they're certainly keen) hoard of fans for whom Christmas won't be Christmas without Cheese Footballs.

All in all we're increasingly fearful about the prospects for Cheese Footballs. At the time of writing they don't appear on either the Jacob's website or that of its parent company United Biscuits, and when we raised questions about them with Jacob's the grim response came back that 'no information on Cheese Footballs can be located'. Is the corporate axe hovering over a much-loved festive favourite? If so, Christmas will never be quite the same again.

KELLOGG'S CORNFLAKES

Considering the vast sums spent on inventing breakfast cereals, it's remarkable that the bestseller of them all came about by accident. Dr John Harvey Kellogg ran a sanitorium in Michigan USA and was looking for a wholesome cereal to give his patients. While experimenting, he found a batch of cooked wheat mush that had been left standing around, and ran it through some rollers. Out of the other end emerged what was to become a global superbrand.

It was his brother William Keith Kellogg who sweetened the flakes with malt and oven-toasted them to perfection. The pair set up a manufacturing company under the unappetizing name of Sanitas. But William was really onto a winner when he switched from toasting wheat to corn. On 19 February 1906, he filed papers incorporating the Battle Creek Toasted Corn Flakes Company – or W.K. Kellogg, as it soon became known.

The first supplies arrived in Britain in the 1920s, and soon gave Force Flakes and Sunny Jim cereals a run for their money. In fact, cornflakes sold so well that a UK factory was opened at Trafford Park, Manchester in 1938. William Keith would surely be impressed if he returned today and could see his flakes tumble-toasting in vast ovens heated by gas flames at 600 degrees C.

The Kellogg's company was also hot on advertising and is said to have spent a million dollars by 1911. The firm is celebrated for its slogans, such as 'The Original and Best', 'Have You Forgotten How Good they Taste?' and, rather dubiously, in 1910, 'Give the Grocer a Wink'.

By Royal appointment

If the crest on the box is to be believed, even Her Majesty chows down to cornflakes in the mornings, or that's certainly what the contents of some distinctly-less-than-regal Tupperware-style containers covertly snapped at Buck House by the *Daily Mirror* looked like. Do you think Charles and Anne used to fight over who got the free toy?

Cornflakes have spawned Bran Flakes, Frosties, Honey Nut Cornflakes and endless competitor products. But we won't go on about which is the healthiest, just read the flippin' box. Wading through that overload of nutritional information should burn up a few calories. Talking of which, why is it that men prefer to sit at the breakfast table reading and re-reading the cereal packet rather than joining in the conversation? And do they really think anyone ever bothered to follow the step-by-step instructions to refold the top of the carton to seal in the freshness?

Oh, and the famous cockerel with the orange beak and bright red comb on the label is called Cornelius. Just about the only fact you won't find printed somewhere on the box.

Survivability	*10/10*
Trolley Embarrassment Factor	*1/10*
Versatility	*LOW*

HEINZ BAKED BEANS

It was probably some half-baked brand manager who suggested changing the spelling of beans to 'beanz' on the label, in homage to the iconic 1960s advertising slogan 'Beanz Means Heinz'. How we laughed. But whatever they now call them, that sweet, slightly glutinous baked bean sauce flows through British bloodstreams. You come home late, you've got the munchies – and baked beans unfailingly do their duty on hot, buttered toast. They add essential lubrication and fibre to bacon, egg, tomato and fried slice. We sit in bathtubs full of them for charity. Even revered Michelin-starred chef Heston Blumenthal couldn't get rid of them when he made over the Little Chef Olympic Breakfast. You could even pretend that they count as one of your 'Five a Day' fruit and veg portions – if you overlook the salt and sugar.

Baked beans became popular around Boston, New England, during the mid-nineteenth century. Haricot beans were soaked, seasoned with mustard, salt-pork and molasses, and taken to local bakery ovens to cook, ready for a Saturday knees-up. Well as much of a knees-up as those bean-eating, God-fearing Puritans could manage. Then someone had the idea of canning the beans (complete with a delicious fatty cube of pork) for the benefit of the New England fishing fleets.

An essential food

But it was the Van Camp Packing Co. of Indianapolis that picked up on the idea of adding tomato to the sauce. The Pittsburgh food company H. J. Heinz wasn't far behind. As early as 1886, its own Baked Beans in Tomato Sauce crossed the Atlantic and arrived on the shelves of Fortnum and Mason's, though it was another forty years before the first factory was opened here.

By the Second World War, baked beans were officially

Survivability	*10/10*
Trolley Embarrassment Factor	*1/10*
Versatility	*LOW*

classified as an 'essential food' – and they have sustained us through adversity ever since. Sales have soared in the face of the global recession. At the last count, we were eating 1.5 million wind-inducing cans of beans every day.

Talking of wind, who can forget that defining scene in the 1974 Mel Brooks movie *Blazing Saddles*, when a bunch of baked-bean-eating cowboys produced an impressive round of flatulence. As to why baked beans give some people gas and not others – well it all apparently depends on your natural intestinal flora.

The biggest threat to Heinz's supremacy has been the advent of Branston baked beans – dreamed up by Premier Foods when it lost the licence to use the HP brand name. Rumour has it that these proved so popular, Heinz had to tweak their own recipe to keep up.

There's a lot of hopscotch in a plate of Heinz Baked Beans

THE BEANS YOU KNOW THEY LOVE
Hop. Skip. Jump. Run. She needs plenty of energy for a game like this. Energy she can get—and to spare—from a meal of Heinz Baked Beans.

Plump, oven-baked beans in the most appetising tomato sauce, rich with the flavour of natural ingredients, prepared in the special Heinz way. So good to eat and so full of good nourishment.

When you give her Heinz Baked Beans, you give her more than just her favourite meal. You give her the help she needs to grow strong and alert and full of life.

Heinz Baked Beans—so good to grow up with

They're beans, Jim ...

Good old baked beans haven't escaped the attentions of the health police – so you can now buy versions with lower salt and sugar, organic beans, beans with added fish oils, hidden vegetables – you name it. For those too idle to wield a tin opener, you'll now find easy ring pulls, microwaveable pots, and baked beans in nosebags for eating on the move (OK, we made that one up).

There is one slightly sinister aspect to the familiar turquoise of the Heinz baked bean tin. Stare at it for long enough to imprint the hue on your brain, then blink or shut your eyes. The colour you will see before you is the opposite one in the spectrum – baked bean colour.

ANGEL DELIGHT

It's easy to forget that before 1967 Planet Pudding was a pretty boring place. Afters was probably jelly or sliced peaches with evaporated milk if you were lucky. So how could anyone forget that first, heavenly experience of Angel Delight, the dessert with an addictively synthetic taste and a light fluffy texture that lingers in the memory? For us, it was right up there with our first hearing of the Beach Boys singing 'Good Vibrations'.

Angel Delight was pure alchemy in a bowl. Rip open the sachet, tip the mixture into a dish, whip it up with milk – and there you have it. Miraculously, a runny liquid turns into a light, smooth mousse before your very eyes – with, as the adverts boldly claimed in 1967, 'the taste of strawberries and cream'. Though let's have no arguments about this – of the half-dozen varieties, butterscotch is the yummiest. Whichever flavour you choose, just remember that when it says there are four servings per pack, this is wildly optimistic. It's perfectly normal for one person to polish off the lot in one go ... isn't it?

Puddings in the space age

In the 1960s, Angel Delight represented the pinnacle of the food technologist's art. This was a pudding for the space age – Prime Minister Harold Wilson's white heat of technology exemplified in a dessert. Even the smell was exciting. Overnight, products you had to make up and leave to set, like blancmange, no longer stood a chance. Only Instant Whip came anything like close.

The stroke of genius was to cut the powdered mixture of sugar and starch with that unique cocktail of tasty emulsifiers, gelling agents, flavourings and whey powder. OK, the ingredients list looks a little scary today (although fortunately it's in very small print), but nobody used to read that stuff then: if anything, Angel Delight was seen as a health food. Serving it was a cunning way to get the kids to drink their milk while simultaneously hiding it from those thieving Humphreys with their red and white-striped drinking straws.

A dessert for little angels

First made by Bird's, Angel Delight was shamelessly targeted at the new time-poor generation of working parents. Why boil a steamed pudding in a cloth for three hours when you could whip this baby up for the kids in the time it took them to watch the ads during *Magpie*?

By the late 1980s, however, nobody could even be bothered to mix up a packet of stuff for tea. Angel Delight was eclipsed by ready-to-eat upstarts like frozen cheesecake, and found itself relegated to division two of the dessert league.

Who knows what the brand owners, Premier Foods, will do with it next. As it is, there have been some pretty deviant varieties in recent years, like candy floss flavour, or adding solid chocolate bits. But we say why stop there? Why not try some modish limited editions? How about Organic Chocolate Chilli, Parma Violets, or a tingly version spiked with Space Dust?

Angel Delight may proclaim itself the 'instant dessert for little angels'. Given our ageing population maybe they should be targeting misty-eyed oldies instead, because it slips down a treat with or without teeth.

Survivability	*10/10*
Trolley Embarrassment Factor	*1/10*
Versatility	*LOW*

KRAFT CHEESE SLICES

For cheese lovers in Britain, 1955 was a memorable year. Before that, cheese had always been pretty recognizable as, well, cheese, but in 1955 the American company Kraft changed all that when it sent a shipment of 'deluxe processed cheese slices' across the Atlantic to the UK. American housewives had been feeding Kraft cheese slices to their families for five years by then and they loved them. In fact, they loved them so much that cheese slices quickly became the most successful

"... swingingest party ever, Mum—and they raved about your Cheese Tropicana"

"Thanks for the party," she said. "That Cheese Tropicana was really gear."

"Too easy," said Mother. "Just lay rolls of ham on a bed of lettuce..."

...take some Kraft Cheese Slices—one for each roll of ham...

... cut the slices into triangles and put them between each roll...

...arrange slices of peeled orange round the edge, serve with Kraft Salad Cream.

"Mum, you're with it," she said. "You must come to the next party you give for me."

Cheese Tropicana EASY TO MAKE WITH
KRAFT DE LUXE CHEESE SLICES CHEESE IS KRAFT
NOW IN FOUR FLAVOURS: CHEDDAR, CHESHIRE, OLD ENGLISH, DANISH BLUE

product the company had ever launched.

Not that this was the first time Kraft had done strange and unnatural things to cheese. Back in 1915 James Lewis Kraft 'changed the cheese landscape', as the company website puts it (and what a wonderful and surreal vision that conjures up) by inventing processed cheese and selling it in tins 'for longer-lasting freshness'. Most of it went to India and Asia, where traditional cheese tended to turn so catastrophically rancid that only the most determined of cheese-eaters could force it down. The next year sales hit $150,000 and the product officially became a runaway success.

Say cheese!

During the First World War, American servicemen masticated their way through more than six million pounds of the stuff (that's pounds in weight, by the way). There was no holding Kraft back after that. Cheese innovation followed cheese innovation, but the boffins really hit the jackpot in the 1940s when they constructed a ground-breaking 'chill roll' apparatus that allowed them to cool hot cheese over a cold drum, turn it into a sheet and slice it into three-inch squares. The cheese slice was born – and consumers couldn't get enough of it.

Nowadays, processed foods are distinctly demode and health conscious consumers prefer to buy authentic, traditionally produced cheeses. But even discerning shoppers

who would sooner disfigure their bathrooms with a crinolined lady toilet-roll cover than embarrass their fridges with a pack of cheese slices, sheepishly admit to enjoying them on a cheeseburger.

Kraft is still *the* name when it comes to processed cheese slices. Blushingly coy about sales figures, rumour has it that the company currently cranks out enough cheese squares every year to pave over Liechtenstein. Or was it Luxembourg? We always get those two muddled up.

Survivability	*8/10*
Trolley Embarrassment Factor	*8/10*
Versatility	*MEDIUM*

CRISPS

Crisps were first invented to annoy somebody. In the summer of 1853, head chef George Crum wanted revenge on a dissatisfied diner at his restaurant in Saratoga Springs, New York. The customer kept sending back his fried potatoes because they were too thick. Irritated, Crum sliced a new batch paper-thin, cooked them to a crisp and leant heavily on the seasoning. Fortunately for both of them, the plan backfired. His customer ate the lot and others began requesting Crum's 'Saratoga Chips'.

The birth of the crisp bag

For years, crisps remained a restaurant speciality – cooked fresh and placed in baskets on the tables. Later they were sold in bins from grocery stores. But the crisps still went soggy, until factory boss Laura Scudder came up with the wheeze of sending women workers home with sheets of waxed paper to iron into packets that could be filled and sealed the next morning. The crisp bag was born.

But it's Frank Smith we have to thank for popularizing crisps in Britain. His was truly a family business – Frank's wife washed, cut and fried the potatoes and he put them in greaseproof bags, which were packed in tins and taken to customers on a pony and trap. By the Second World War, Smiths Crisps was the brand leader. It's said that, during wartime, women packers would sometimes slip little notes with their names and addresses inside the bags, in case they were read by lonely soldiers. Sadly, Smiths failed to hold on to its market share, and was eventually merged with what was once just an upstart regional brand – Walkers. The founder, Henry Walker, was a successful Midlands pork butcher. But when post-war rationing made meat scarce, his company took to producing crisps in a fish fryer above its butchery in Oxford Street, Leicester. Walkers never looked back.

Survivability	*10/10*
Trolley Embarrassment Factor	*7/10*
Versatility	*LOW*

The little blue twist

If you've ever wondered why plain crisps are called 'ready salted', well that's down to Golden Wonder, who figured out how to dispense with the little twist of salt in blue paper. We're told that sometimes there was an extra blue salt bag by mistake – quite a hazard if you took crisps to the pictures as, in the dark, people used to swallow the blue bag by mistake.

Today, crisps must be the world's favourite snack – but that's not necessarily a good thing. Instead of sitting down to savour the potato flavour and the crunchy texture as part of a meal, we just grab handfuls at the bar to soak up the alcohol – or absentmindedly feed our faces with our own weight

Salt-free crisps.
(With bags of salt.)

If you're trying to cut down on salt you don't need to cut out crisps.

Salt 'n'Shake are the first salt-free crisps. They're deliciously crunchy but they're definitely not salty. Unless, of course, you want them to be. We've put the salt in a little blue bag so you can choose just how much (or little) you want. Ingenious isn't it? And exclusive to Smiths.

SMITHS

SMITHs Salt n'Shake CRISPs

TO SALT OR NOT TO SALT
THE CHOICE IS YOURS

in crisps while we watch TV. No wonder the British Heart Foundation warned that half of UK children 'drink' almost five litres of cooking oil every year just from their crisp intake.

What's your favourite flavour?

As for flavours, it was an Irish crisp company, Tayto, who invented the technology to produce flavoured crisps. But it's still the Walkers company that is wilfully ignoring the international conventions for crisp packet colours. Just to confuse us, it insists on putting salt-and-vinegar in green packets and cheese-and-onion in blue. Apparently, it was a deliberate ploy that succeeded in getting many more people to try the salt-and-vinegar flavour.

You can also argue a long time about the merits of different varieties – is there really

MAKE THE MOST OF **SMITH'S CRISPS**

Smith's Crisps are delicious straight from the packet and popular with everyone . . . but there are hundreds of other ways in which they can be used.

Try them for cooking - as delicious 'topping for casseroles crushed in pastry for pieshells - as a crunchy contrast to ragouts and fricassées.

Try them as 'dips' with cream cheese, barbecue sauces and fondues. They make the perfect spoon, easy to serve, easy to handle and gorgeous to eat!

Try them as canapé bases with anchovies, egg, asparagus and smoked salmon, or pâté. They make a light, crisp tit-bit for cocktail savouries.

Crisps hot, crisps cold, crisps in cooking— write for a recipe leaflet today and see in how many ways Smith's Crisps can make your cooking more exciting. Always keep a Family Pack of Smith's Crisps in your kitchen.

SMITH'S POTATO CRISPS LTD.,
Great West Road, Brentford, Middlesex.

some kind of addictive substance in prawn cocktail? Why are smoky bacon sometimes tasty, but sometimes revolting? – though perhaps we can all agree that, however nice they are, no way do chicken-flavoured crisps taste like chicken. As for today's ever-fancier flavours, well you're welcome to the short-lived, sensory overload to be gained from scoffing Thai sweet chilli or Cajun-squirrel flavoured crisps. For us, nothing can beat the delights of a layer of our favourite crisps in a white sliced bread buttie – tomato ketchup or Marmite optional.

PAXO STUFFING

Survivability	**7/10**
Trolley Embarrassment Factor	**6/10**
Versatility	**LOW**

Until the 1980s, the word 'stuffing' was virtually synonymous with Paxo. Hardly anyone made their own, and despite the best efforts of Delia, Jamie, Nigella *et al*, all those delicious concoctions carefully prepared using organic sausage meat, fresh herbs and dried fruit still don't taste like stuffing to many people brought up on Paxo.

It was John Crampton, a butcher from Eccles, who invented the product in 1901. He apparently thought the addition of some sage and onion might make Sunday lunches 'more exciting', which gives us a pretty good idea of just how dull the conversation must have been *chez* Crampton. Being a man who firmly believes that stuffing should be made from scratch and chickens treated with respect, Hugh Fearnley-Whittingstall will be doubly annoyed to hear that it was battery farming that really got Paxo off the ground. Crampton's product chugged along reasonably successfully for about fifty years but poultry was too expensive for ordinary folk to buy on a regular basis and sales were far from spectacular. By the 1950s, however, British farmers were beginning to copy the intensive rearing methods already used in Russia. Poultry prices fell sharply, roast chicken stopped being a special occasion luxury and quickly became a weekly family tradition. Paxo sales shot up.

Stuffing with everything

Even now, when many supermarkets sell delicious fresh stuffing, nearly one in three British households still tuck into Paxo at least once a year because 'Christmas', as the ads have been telling us for years, 'wouldn't be Christmas without the Paxo'. And if you tend to agree but can't summon up the energy to actually cook a turkey of your own, don't worry, because Walkers recently launched a Christmas edition of Roast Turkey Crisps with Paxo Sage and Onion. Problem solved.

TINNED SALMON

We well remember making tinned salmon sandwiches as a special occasion treat when we were children. It was rather a laborious business because If you didn't dissect the contents of the can with the skill of a brain surgeon someone always ended up with an alarming mouthful of crunchy vertebrae. But once they had been carefully extracted – along with the skin if you were really picky – it only took a splash of vinegar and a sprinkle of salt and pepper from the kitchen cruet (no one owned salt and pepper mills back then) and you were ready to tackle the delicate task of sharing out what never seemed quite enough salmon between rather too many slices of white, buttered bread.

Fish in a basket

The first tinned salmon was supposedly produced in Aberdeen in 1824. But it was fifty years later, on the majestic Columbia River, which runs 2,000 kilometres down from Canada to the Pacific Ocean on the Oregon-Washington border, that salmon canning really took off, largely thanks to a man called William

How can you tell which is the best canned salmon?

With ordinary salmon you have to wait till you open the can before you see what you are getting. But when you see the name John West's on the label you know at once that here is the finest of all red Salmon, a rich appetising colour, tender, juicy, flaky and nourishing.

Always . . . insist on the best and buy John West's.

JOHN WEST'S
"Middle-Cut" Brand
SALMON

Hume. William and his three brothers grew up in Maine, where seafood canning was already a flourishing business, and when he visited California as a young man he quickly saw there was money to be made out of all those fat salmon in the Sacramento River. In 1864 he set up his first cannery and started selling his tinned fish door-to-door from a basket. Less than twenty years later, canned salmon was selling worldwide on a huge scale, and by the time William died in 1902, his cannery on the Columbia River was producing nearly half a million cases a year and salmon canning had spread to Canada, Alaska and Japan and was about to take off in Siberia.

Unsurprisingly, the salmon population couldn't keep up. Worldwide demand was enormous, especially during the First World War, and from the 1920s onwards, Pacific wild fish stocks rapidly fell away, decimated by over-fishing and pollution. In 1980 the last major cannery on the river finally closed down.

Red, red salmon

Modern shoppers like their salmon to be as red as possible, which is why red salmon is more expensive than pink. This is also why salmon farmers controversially feed their fish artificial colourings to turn them a stronger hue, and – much like anxious home-decorators – even use colour charts to help them pick the exact shade they're after. Despite their efforts though, most of us now prefer tuna.

A final word of advice: thanks to their couch-potato lifestyle, farmed salmon can contain as much fat as bacon, while their lean, mean, ocean-going cousins have less than two per cent. And yes, if it really bothers you that much, you can now buy tinned salmon without any skin and bones. Apparently older people aren't bothered, but manufacturers have discovered that younger people won't buy it *au naturel*. Wimps. If their grandparents don't mind picking the bones out of their dentures what are they complaining about?

Survivability	*6/10*
Trolley Embarrassment Factor	*5/10*
Versatility	*HIGH*

CAMP COFFEE

Given that it's just a blend of chicory, coffee, sugar and water, Camp Coffee has a surprisingly gripping history. It was invented in the 1870s by a Scottish company called R. Paterson & Sons, which, about a hundred years later, was bought out by the spice manufacturers Schwartz, and then became part of the giant American seasonings empire McCormick & Company. Not that McCormick makes anything of the fact; at the time of writing there's no mention of Camp on the US or UK websites.

This coyness may or may not have something to do with the fact that Camp Coffee was the focus of some doubtless less-than-welcome press attention a few years ago, when its famous label was condemned by race equality campaigners. The original label featured a Sikh servant bringing a cup of Camp Coffee, on a tray, to his kilted master. In due course, the tray disappeared from the servant's hand, and the current version depicts the two men sitting down together as equals, each with his own cup of coffee. The makers refused to link the controversy to the re-design, but the change was welcomed by The Central Scotland Racial Equality Council, not to mention certain shopkeepers who were threatening to boycott the product.

Suicide in Paris

Camp Coffee came into being in rather unusual circumstances. In the 1870s, a Glaswegian sauce and ketchup manufacturer called Campbell Paterson received an unexpected request from The Gordon Highlanders, a Scottish regiment then serving in India: the officers were great devotees of coffee, but grinding and brewing the real stuff just wasn't practical in a field kitchen – could Paterson help? He put his thinking cap on and came up with 'Camp'. The first instant coffee was born.

The soldier depicted on the label is believed to be Major

Survivability	*1/10*
Trolley Embarrassment Factor	*7/10*
Versatility	*MEDIUM*

General Sir Hector Macdonald, an exceptionally brave officer of the Gordon Highlanders. Macdonald, the son of a Ross-shire crofter, rose from the ranks after distinguishing himself in battle in Afghanistan in 1879. Having turned down a Victoria Cross in favour of a commission, 'Fighting Mac' went on to become a national hero after his exploits at the Battle of Omdurman. Sadly, after an illustrious career, he shot himself in a Paris hotel bedroom in 1903 on reading in the *New York Herald* that a 'grave charge' – almost certainly homosexuality – was to be brought against him. Whether there was any truth in the suggestion is hotly contested to this day, but he left a wife Christina (whom he had secretly married in

Give yourself a break . . .

A little rest gives you a lot of energy. So relax, and have a cup of 'Camp'.

'Camp' is so quick, so simple. Just put a teaspoonful of 'Camp' into a cup of hot milk and water and a refreshing drink is ready for your enjoyment.

The secret of 'Camp' is skilful blending of fine coffee, chicory and pure cane sugar. 'Camp' is economical, too. It is so concentrated that you need only a little and so a bottle lasts longer. There is no waste with 'Camp'—and you have only the cup to wash up.

have a cup of 'CAMP'

PER BOTTLE
Small size 1/5½d.
Large size 2/8d.
Café size 4/5d.

defiance of Lord Kitchener, who preferred his officers to remain bachelors) and a son.

Café chic

Camp and other liquid coffee essences were hugely popular during the Second World War; they were easy to make and, importantly, already sweetened, so they didn't eat into the sugar ration. Coffee drinking really took off around that time, not least because its popularity with American servicemen lent it a certain glamour. After the war, powdered instant coffees began to take over and nowadays Camp Coffee can be hard to find; ask for it in a supermarket and unless the assistant is perilously close to his or her pension you'll probably get a blank look. Most of the people who do buy it use it as a cooking ingredient and there's a lot to be said for it in a coffee cake. Some hardy souls may even still drink it – there's no accounting for taste.

LYLE'S GOLDEN SYRUP

Question: is anything sweeter than sugar? Answer: yes, Lyle's Golden Syrup. Apparently this is a scientific fact, although the details really are a bit technical. Suffice to say that 'partially inverted sugar' (that's what golden syrup is) is very sweet indeed and its devotees are the sort of patients who make dentists rub their hands with glee and start leafing through exotic holiday brochures.

Having an ancient tin of Golden Syrup stuck to the shelf at the back of a kitchen cupboard is a fine and long-established British tradition. So what if you sprain your wrist wrenching it free and have to raid the tool box for an implement man enough to prize the lid off? There really is something magical about the sight and smell of that fragrant gold tsunami slowly sliding from one side of the tilted tin to the other, and there's even more pleasure to be had from loading up a spoon and watching it cascade languorously over your porridge, although this is not something to do if you're pressed for time.

Selling by the ton

In the 1880s there were more than seventy sugar refineries on the banks of the river Thames, but none of them produced golden syrup until Scottish entrepreneur Abram Lyle came on the scene. The plan was to open yet another refinery but competition was tough and they hit problems. The solution was the bright idea to sell 'goldie' – a gooey by-product of the refining process, which was usually wasted. People loved it, shops clamoured for dispensers to sell it, and Lyle was soon selling a ton a week.

Lyle merged with a Thameside rival, Tate, in 1921, creating an enterprise that processed half of Britain's sugar and operated the largest cane sugar refinery in the world. For reasons best known to themselves the two sides kept their distance and their

Survivability	*10/10*
Trolley Embarrassment Factor	*1/10*
Versatility	*HIGH*

own specialities, Lyle's opposite number Henry Tate being famed for his sugar cubes. It's even said that the two sugar barons never met in person, nor did their respective families enter each other's factories.

Tate later turned to philanthropy, and turned himself into a household name to this day by famously endowing the Tate Gallery at Millbank in London.

Squeezy vs tinned

Today Tate & Lyle is a global player, and every month, the Plaistow refinery turns out more than a million tins of what's one of our most widely recognized exports. As for the dead lion on the tin, it was Abram Lyle himself who came up with the undeniably odd tableau taken from the bible story of Samson. If he was alive today we suspect he'd be something of a pub quiz devotee because he seems to have been trying to create some sort of pictorial riddle. Quite what it had to do with selling syrup is anybody's guess – but it worked.

PICCALILLI

Piccalilli is a hot topic among a small but vocal element in the foodie world. Rather like Marmite, this fluorescent yellow pickle is one of those foods that tend to provoke a violent response. Sadly, unlike Marmite, it's fair to say that fans of piccalilli are heavily outnumbered by those who simply cannot understand why anyone would want to obliterate the flavour of a nice slice of cold beef with such an aggressive condiment. The sad fact is that despite the great British love affair with curry, for most people Piccalilli is a step too far.

Show me the cauli

In an attempt to win back sales, some manufacturers have cravenly toned down their recipes by easing back on the mustard and turmeric and adding more sugar. Equally regrettably, some have also tinkered with the traditional rough-cut texture. Time was when you could see the cauliflower and green beans jostling for position in the jar, but modern versions tend to involve neatly cubed and unidentifiable vegetables suspended in a smooth yellow sauce – a far cry from the feisty, full-on chewing experience you could once expect.

Contemporary recipes vary, but they invariably involve cauliflower, which may well be part of the problem. If anyone can think of a more unfashionable vegetable than the cauliflower we'd be glad to hear of it. Undeservedly, it now seems to be universally reviled and exasperated farmers are ditching the crop, warning that homegrown cauli could soon disappear completely. But if piccalilli-makers do have to start importing cauliflower from far-flung places such as Thailand it'll be full circle for mustard pickle.

You say potato...

Its roots lie thousands of miles away in the jars of 'Achar', or pickled fruit and vegetables, which seventeenth-century European sailors used to buy in India to take on sea voyages. By the late 1700s, British housewives had taken to making their own and the first recorded recipe is by a Mrs Raffald in 1772. Her 'Piccalillo' used commonly available vegetables such as cauliflower, cabbage, cucumber, kidney beans and beetroot but

Survivability	*3/10*
Trolley Embarrassment Factor	*1/10*
Versatility	*LOW*

earlier cooks make mention of 'Indian pickle' made with the trademark mustard powder and turmeric too.

Already blessed with a charming name, piccalilli was also known in the nineteenth century as 'English Chow Chow', which may have had something to do with the French word for cabbage. A much-loved staple in Southern States cooking even now, Chow Chow is widely but erroneously believed by the locals to have arrived with immigrant Chinese railroad workers in the 1800s. Mind you, everyone has tried to take the credit for mustard pickle over there; the Amish, Mennonite and Pennsylvania Dutch communities all cook it up to this day, just as they've been doing since the 1600s. Suffice to say that Crosse & Blackwell sell 'Chow Chow' in America and 'Piccalilli' over here because, as everybody knows, the customer is always right.

BRANSTON PICKLE

We Brits still love to bring out the Branston and never more so than around Christmas when six million jars are sold, pushing global sales to over 28 million jars every year. That's an awful lot of pickle by anyone's standards.

Cheddar cheese or cold meat with Branston on the side is classic Sunday-evening Britnosh. And come Monday morning, what else are you going to find in the fridge to cheer up a hastily made sandwich?

The pickle crisis

Some reports say the original Branston Pickle recipe came from a Mrs Graham and her daughters, who used to cook it up in their kitchen at Branston village, Staffordshire. Mrs Graham is said to have had an interest in biological research, which could explain the array of relatively exotic ingredients like gherkins and dates. The first jars rattled off the food producers' Crosse and Blackwell production line in 1922 – the factory used to be within the Branston parish, just outside Burton. The founders, Edmund Crosse and Thomas Blackwell had a Royal Warrant and a long history of acquiring successful recipes. Production moved in turn from Staffordshire to Derbyshire and now is at Bury St Edmunds, Suffolk. The darkest hour for Branston was the so-called 'Pickle Crisis' of 2004, when a swish new factory burned down. A few jars were auctioned on ebay, but the world was never at serious risk of running out of Branston.

Catherine Zeta-Jones is a fan, and once sent her husband Michael Douglas out for a jar. It's hard to imagine which was more challenging for him – trying to locate a jar of Branston in downtown LA, or having to do the shopping himself. For the rest of us, sitting outside a pub on a sunny day with a Ploughman's Lunch of cheddar cheese, crusty bread and Branston Pickle is one of life's simplest pleasures. But don't get too carried away with that nostalgic vision – documents uncovered at the National Archive reveal that the term 'Ploughman's Lunch' was invented by the

Milk Marketing Board in 1960 as a ploy to sell English cheese in pubs.

Branston with no bits

Branston has done its level best to broaden the pickle spectrum. If you're a wuss and can't cope with the big veggie chunks, well that's no excuse because there's now a Branston with tiny, weeny bits that won't fall out of your sarnies. Another version is entirely pulped – all the familiar taste, but, disconcertingly, none of the texture. Branston also sells baked beans but – confusingly – they don't taste of Branston.

Branston really is the business when it comes to sweet pickle – somehow, its rivals can't quite match the vinegary bite of those tangy pickled vegetables in that complex-tasting, slightly glutinous sweet brown sauce. As with pickling itself, there really is some combination of art, science and magic involved, when you consider that you can open a jar that's been sitting on a

Pick the best – pick a tasty mixture of goodness. Onions. Carrots. Tomatoes. Marrow. Apples. Gherkin. And more. Take them and turn them into a pickle that is all flavour. The pick of pickles. A bottleful of Branston. for your table. Pick Crosse & Blackwell BRANSTON PICKLE

shelf for months and find the contents still fresh and crunchy. Allow it all to linger on your tongue and you can savour the dates, gherkins, cauliflower and carrots, with a nice background kick from the spices. But we bet you won't recognize the second largest named ingredient on the jar – rutabaga. Wow – a vegetable no one has even heard of? In fact, there's less to this than meets the eye: rutabaga is just the American name for swede. What a swiz.

Survivability	*9/10*
Trolley Embarrassment Factor	*2/10*
Versatility	*LOW*

TWIGLETS

What's your favourite Italian food? Pasta? Pizza? Twiglets? Yes, it's one of those 'strange but true' facts that perhaps this most quintessentially British of cocktail snacks was invented by a Piedmontese named Laurent Rondolin. The year was 1929 and Signore Rondolin was working for the Peak Frean's biscuit factory in Bermondsey when inspiration struck. Cannily using the same dough that was used for the company's Vitawheat crispbread, he experimented with various shapes and recipes before lighting on the unlikely – but winning – formula of a knobbly twig, flavoured with yeast extract.

Launched in time for the Christmas market that same year, Twiglets were sold in boxes until the mid 1980s when Jacob's Bakery relegated them to bags. Apparently the company wanted us to buy Twiglets more frequently as an alternative to crisps, and not just as a cocktail party snack. This was a sound idea because only about twelve people had actually held a cocktail party since

1973. Sales rose dramatically. Still going strong today Twiglets are now marketed as a wholegrain, high-fibre snack, with the added advantage that they're baked rather than fried – a powerful weapon on the snack-food battleground. As the obesity message is hammered home to consumers, manufacturers are casting around for anything that might help us feel a little less guilty about munching on junk foods.

While the flavour of Twiglets has hardly changed in eighty-odd years, longstanding fans complain that they are now shorter and less knobbly than they used to be. Nowhere near as much fun to eat as a genuinely 'twiggy' Twiglet.

Survivability	*7/10*
Trolley Embarrassment Factor	*3/10*
Versatility	*LOW*

TETLEY TEA BAGS

Napoleon may have reckoned Britain was a nation of shopkeepers, but first and foremost we're a nation of tea-drinkers. Joseph Tetley & Co brought paper tea bags to Britain in 1953, and doggedly stuck with the idea until tea drinkers came round to it. Now, OK, a few people still get up in the morning, boil the kettle, warm the pot, measure out the tea leaves, wait while the tea brews, strain it into a cup and finally drink it before tackling the unlovely job of washing everything up and clearing soggy tea leaves out of the kitchen plughole. For the rest of us, tea bags are one of those truly clever inventions that genuinely make life easier. Even the UK Tea Council has admitted the innovation saved the industry, which was starting to worry about the

competition from instant coffee. Needless to say, a proper pot of Earl Grey is perfect for a Sunday afternoon, or for when the vicar pops round (do vicars pop round unannounced any more?).

Spawn of the devil

The initial response to tea bags may have been tepid, but once they came up with those little perforations, the Tetley Tea Folk never looked back. Now, only four per cent of the 130 million cups we down every day are made from loose-leaf tea. Though, funnily enough, we all know someone who has doggedly held out for the last fifty years – swearing that tea bags are the spawn of the devil and are only filled with sweepings from the tea factory floor. In fact, the bag contains CTC leaves, which means they are crushed, torn and curled by machine to ensure a strong and rapid, if less subtle, brew.

Tea bags are another product that was invented by accident. The story goes that a New York merchant, Thomas

Survivability	*10/10*
Trolley Embarrassment Factor	*3/10*
Versatility	*LOW*

Sullivan, was annoyed at the high cost of tin tea boxes, so in 1908 he sent out his samples in little hand-sewn silk bags. But his penny-pinching was misconstrued and customers just starting dropping the bags into hot water. Unfortunately, Sullivan never took out a patent and many others took up the idea, experimenting with materials like gauze, cheesecloth and cellophane before plumping for paper fibre.

Convenient or not, the idea was slow to cross the Atlantic. Perhaps it was a lot to do with the quality of the dusty tea some makers used over there, combined with the lax American habit of just waving the bag in a cup of lukewarm water. It's much the same reason why the British order tea on the Continent at their peril. Both of us remember our mothers moaning about the tea on holiday; now we have to resist the temptation to do the same ourselves.

Makers desperately want to differentiate their brands and the most notable design innovation over the years has been the introduction of round or pyramid-shaped bags. It just seems hard to believe that any improvement in tea bag circulation efficiency is more than marginal.

Tea for the new age

Now part of the Tata Group of India, Tetley is the market leader, and has an impressive array of products – including today's trendy Redbush and green tea varieties. But come on, let's just say it, there is something slightly annoying about people who refuse a nice cup of your 'builders brew' and then make you feel inadequate because you don't have their favourite new-age blend of peppermint, lemon and ginger, rosehip or camomile. Whichever varieties you stock up on, you never seem to have the right one.

It may be an affront to the traditional tea-drinker, but all the major brands have read their tea leaves and are moving into this market. Mind you, if PG Tips need to advertise herbal tea in future, goodness knows what they'll have to spike it with to get those naughty chimps to drink it.

TUNNOCK'S TEACAKES

What makes something hip? While it's somehow obvious why some things will never be hip (men's hockey, Crocs on anyone over 4 ft 6 in tall, malt loaf), it's trickier to work out why certain, often unlikely, products mysteriously are. Tunnock's Teacakes are a case in point. Beloved by the likes of Coldplay's Chris Martin, they're the chocolate snack of choice in hip hotel mini-bars from Antigua to Zimbabwe.

Cooler than cool

Maybe it's the retro packaging – that red and silver foil is reassuring in a solid, Thomas-the-Tank-Engine sort of way that own-brand versions can't match. Or maybe it's their lush plumpness? The oblong Caramel Wafers made by the same

Survivability	*9/10*
Trolley Embarrassment Factor	*3/10*
Versatility	*LOW*

company may sell better, but for us they can't compete with the curvaceous charms of a Teacake. Much has also been written about the delicate consistency of the marshmallow used by Tunnock's, which apparently contains egg white and is considered by aficionados to be superior to the gelatine-based version found in other brands. Perhaps it's because 'Tunnock's' sounds like a word invented at a marketing meeting but isn't; or because Uddingston, where the factory stands, is such a comical name for a town; or even because it's so odd that they're called Teacakes when they're nothing of the sort. Whatever the reason, they're uber-cool and Boyd Tunnock's company turns out three million of them every week in a factory just fifty yards from the little shop where his grandfather Thomas Tunnock founded the business in 1890.

A cure for homesickness

Marshmallow itself is far older than that, in fact it's believed to be one of the earliest confections known to man, and was originally made from the root sap of the marshmallow herb, but it was the French who produced the first recognizable marshmallow creations around 1850. Tunnock's chocolate-covered contribution to the marshmallow diaspora was launched a century later, alongside Caramel Logs, Caramel Wafers and Snowballs (similar to Teacakes but covered in grated coconut and strictly for people with too much time on their hands, because you have to pick the stuff out of your teeth afterwards). But it was the Teacakes that quickly became iconic throughout Scotland. The current chief, Boyd Tunnock CBE has three daughters and a son-in-law all working in the business, and their products are exported worldwide. Word has it that demand is highest in the Middle East, because of all the Scottish oil workers out there who depend on Tunnock's treats to fend off homesickness.

Traditional almost to a fault, Tunnock's have made a few concessions to modern tastes, such as the plain chocolate-covered Teacakes that are now on offer in a blue and gold version of the traditional Teacake livery. Happily, despite the razzmatazz of visiting rock stars (Supergrass even made a pilgrimage to the factory to see Teacakes being made) and tales of vodka-fuelled Teacake-eating competitions at LA pool parties, a delightfully homely eccentricity persists at the factory. Across the road you can find the tearoom, an establishment justly famed for its captivating window displays of figures constructed out of Tunnock's own products. Imagine an owl with a Teacake body and hand-painted wooden wings and legs and you're getting the picture. Irresistible.

NIMBLE

It was all so much simpler when, in the words of that horribly catchy TV ad, Maggie the Nimble girl could 'fly like a bird in the sky' nibbling on her Nimble sandwich. Back then, if you were feeling a bit podgy you just bought a low-calorie version of your favourite food. The makers made sales so they were happy, and hopefully you were too when you lost a few pounds. Now, despite all those headlines about the obesity plague sweeping across the western world, diet foods are having a thinner time of it.

Only recently, the industry was confidently expecting sales to carry on growing every year but it's just not happening. Why? Because today's consumers know there's more to healthy eating than just calorie-counting and more of them are choosing to exercise and eat carefully instead of resorting to highly processed low-cal products.

Never slow to cash in on a lucrative trend, the supermarkets have all launched their own 'healthy eating' ranges, leaving many of the traditional diet food manufacturers running to catch up.

Burning off the bulge

In Maggie's day, women were expected to 'look after their figures' but men could eat what they liked. And fifty years ago, Brits of both sexes tucked away far more calories than we do now. Unlike us, however, they also burned them off; central heating was a luxury, manual labourers outnumbered office workers, car ownership was low and couch potatoes didn't exist. Dieting for men was virtually unheard of and women who wanted to shed a few pounds simply ate less of everything until they'd achieved the desired result.

By the 1950s, however, dieting was becoming popular in the States and even Marilyn Monroe was photographed jogging. Special diet foods, including a low-calorie bread called Procea (a forerunner to Slimcea), began to emerge here in the UK. With the 1960s came the first twig-thin supermodel, and diet fever hit Britain. Women flocked to the new slimming clubs, Weight Watchers and Slimming World, and low-calorie breads took off in a big way. Nimble, then part of the Rank Hovis McDougall stable, went head-to-head

Real bread — but lighter

with its arch rival Slimcea and before long they were slugging it out with what were to become iconic TV campaigns. Remember the Nimble girl in her hot-air balloon? And the Sunsilk blonde showing us 'she was a Slimcea girl'?

Light and delicious recipes with Nimble bread...

ABERDEEN SCRAMBLE
2 servings

2 slices of Nimble (toasted)
4 oz. cooked smoked haddock
4 eggs
Seasoning
Chopped parsley (if available)
¼ oz. butter

Flake fish, add to beaten eggs with seasoning and parsley. Heat butter in saucepan, add fish and egg mixture and cook gently, stirring until mixture has lightly scrambled. Serve on Nimble toast.
Approx. 360 calories a serving

SUNSHINE TOMATOES
2 servings

2 slices Nimble (toasted)
2 large tomatoes
2 eggs
Seasoning

Cut 'lid' off the tomatoes and scoop out the interior and season inside. Break egg into tomato case. Replace lid. Bake in a moderate oven (Gas No. 4—350°F.) for about 25 minutes until egg is lightly set. Serve on buttered toast.
Approx. 220 calories a serving.

So many diets are based on substitutes for proper food. Nimble is delicious, real fresh bread, but bread baked lighter so it's designed to fit neatly into a calorie-controlled diet—and so to help you slim.

But because Nimble tastes so good, it's bread that the whole family will enjoy—especially toasted for breakfast—yet one slice of Nimble contains only 40 calories, compared to 67 for ordinary bread.

NEW
Nimble
only 40 calories a slice

Nimble is a lovely way to slim

Survivability	*2/10*
Trolley Embarrassment Factor	*10/10*
Versatility	*MEDIUM*

The 'O-word'

Low-cal breads fell out of fashion in the 1980s and 1990s, overtaken by faddish celebrity diets and, more recently, the trend towards sensible eating. Not that it's working: the percentage of obese people has almost doubled since the 1980s and the 'O word' now officially applies to about a quarter of us. Women may obsess more than ever about their weight but it seems that most men remain unconcerned about their ever-expanding waistlines. In 2007 Nimble followed up its fiftieth anniversary with its first TV campaign in twenty years. In a complete reversal of traditional strategy, it targeted men, featuring a tasty, if slightly overweight, builder. After his wife secretly swapped his usual sandwich bread for Nimble he lost so much weight that his trousers kept falling down. Since the campaign was linked to a Nimble survey that suggested that women could perk up their sex lives by encouraging their men to lose weight, this was presumably exactly what she had in mind.

And talking of rejuvenation, it has to be said that a slice of modern Nimble does look more appealing than the flaccid white thing it used to be. It's thicker, high fibre, and you can buy a wholemeal or malted wholegrain version if you want to – all at less than fifty calories a slice. On the other hand, it's no longer possible to while away an idle moment by compressing it to see just how thin it will go and folding it up. We don't know what they've done to it, but it's just too springy. Sorry.

ROSE'S LIME CORDIAL

Rose's Lime Cordial may hold a Royal Warrant, but stripped of its beautiful lime leaf-embossed glass bottle, it's a shadow of its elegant former self. True, it's still to be found nestling up to the Triple Sec and the Angostura Bitters in cocktail bars the world over, but clad in a cheap plastic bottle Rose's looks more Romford than Riviera these days and classy she ain't.

Off your face on the ocean waves

Not, it has to be admitted, that Rose's began life as a posh drink – far from it. Scurvy sailors were the first consumers of Rose's lime, or at least they would have been scurvy if they hadn't drunk it. In 1867 a Scottish juice merchant named Lauchlin Rose patented a method of preserving lime juice, which stopped it fermenting on long voyages. Happily for him, The Merchant Shipping Act of the same year made it compulsory for all Royal Navy and Merchant Navy ships to provide a daily lime ration, and his company made a killing providing them with the necessary supplies. The men on the receiving end, however, were less happy. Before Rose came along and spoiled things they were given their juice preserved in rum and although Whitehall would have preferred the nation's sailors to stay sober at sea, the sailors themselves had other ideas. They turned to gin to wash down their lime ration and the story goes that a naval surgeon in the 1870s named T. O. Gimlette was the man behind the Gimlet cocktail.

MORNING'S AT SEVEN

SITTING her horse with easy confidence, this young rider is off for an early morning canter across the downs. When she tells you that only last night she threw a very lively party, you may wonder at her sparkling eyes and radiant complexion. The solution is a very simple one : she always insists on Rose's Lime Juice with her gin. She knows that thanks to Rose's she will keep the slender figure that fashion demands and greet the morning with happy memories of the night before.

Gin and **ROSE'S LIME JUICE**
The man's drink that women appreciate

The cocktail set

Meanwhile, Rose's had begun to sell its cordial to the public in its distinctive lime leaf bottle. In 1895 the company bought into a lime plantation on Dominica in the Caribbean and soon began exporting to the US. By the 1920s the company was flourishing, the cocktail era was in full swing and Rose's was established as an essential ingredient that no self-respecting barman or sophisticated hostess could afford to be without. In 1957 the Rose family sold out to Schweppes and in 1988, still riding high with ninety-nine per cent of US lime juice sales, Rose's changed hands again, this time to Texas-

Survivability	*7/10*
Trolley Embarrassment Factor	*3/10*
Versatility	*MEDIUM*

A CRICKETER'S FAREWELL

"Goodbye, old willow. No more thy flashing blade shall smack the crimson leather to the distant boundary . . ."

"What the dickens are you up to?"

"I'm writing a farewell ode to my bat. After the performance I gave this afternoon I feel I ought to take up croquet. There were so many spots before my eyes I didn't know which one to take a crack at."

"A celebration last night I presume. If you had taken the precaution of mixing Rose's Lime Juice with your gin your hand would be as steady as a middle stump in the tea interval."

"Excellent advice my friend, what's wrong with a large gin and Rose's now?"

ROSE'S — *for Gin and Lime*

based drinks giant the Dr Pepper Snapple Group.

Here in the UK, Rose's lime cordial is sold under licence, along with Rose's marmalades. Since fresh limes became readily available its popularity has faded. Marmalade too is struggling – apparently many children have no idea what it is – and the makers have even toyed with the idea of renaming it 'orange jam'. No wonder Paddington Bear is putting Marmite in his sandwiches nowadays.

LUCOZADE

Lucozade might still have been claiming to 'aid recovery' in the late 1970s, but in reality it was dying on its feet. Public health was improving, flu epidemics were less frequent and the yellow-cellophane-wrapped bottle looked exactly what it was – dated. Sales started falling off a cliff – down a third in just four years – and, at the ripe old age of fifty, Lucozade was in serious need of resuscitation. It was all a far cry from the 1950s and 60s, when the fizzy glucose-rich drink was Beecham's bestselling line and appeared in pretty well every sickroom or hospital ward worthy of the name.

Drink up, it'll do you good

If you're over fifty, Lucozade will inevitably remind you of when you were ill. That was, after all, the only time you drank it, in the firm belief that it would help you to get better. Someone was despatched to the chemist and the important-looking bottle was purchased and ceremonially brought to your bedside. After a build-up like that, the weak taste of the original Lucozade was always a disappointment, but in some mystical way this all seemed part of the cure.

An attempt to persuade housewives to drink Lucozade as a pick-me-up fizzled out, but it did prepare the ground for a radical idea: marketing Lucozade to people who weren't actually ill! Fired up with the sales limitations of only selling to the sick, Beechams relaunched Lucozade with a wide-mouthed bottle and a new line, 'Lucozade replaces lost energy'. It was hardly the most inspired advertising copywriting in the world and it failed to make much of a dent in the lucrative carbonated drinks market Beechams wanted to crack. Coke and Pepsi were the big sellers at the time and Lucozade, far from being a hip alternative, was still viewed by younger consumers as something their mums used to give them when they were poorly.

With a little help from Iron Maiden

The breakthrough came in the early 1980s, with the bright

idea to link Lucozade's energy-boosting qualities to sporting excellence. Beechams signed up athlete Daley Thompson and a compelling TV ad featuring him in motion against an Iron Maiden soundtrack did the trick. Sales rocketed by forty per cent in the first year of the campaign. Lucozade was back.

Now part of the pharmaceutical colossus GlaxoSmithKline, Lucozade has diversified into a bewildering variety of energy and sports products. Thanks to twenty more years of concerted marketing spend, it's also inextricably bound up in the public consciousness with sporting events from Premier League football to the London Marathon, slugging it out with the likes of Red Bull and its old enemies Pepsi and Coke in supermarkets and garage forecourts the world over.

It's all a long way from 1927 when, the story goes, Lucozade was created on Tyneside by chemist William

ade
The sparkling
GLUCOSE drink

the jaded appetite — the refreshing sparkle of
[L]UCOZADE is irresistible. Parents are deeply im-
[pres]sed by the way children take to LUCOZADE —
[will]ingly, eagerly, when other foods may have been
[refu]sed. To help in building up children's vitality —
[giv]e them this exciting, refreshing drink. And then
[wat]ch them lift up their little faces for more. Once
[tas]ted, LUCOZADE is never refused.
[L]UCOZADE is used extensively in CLINICS,
[H]OSPITALS, NURSING HOMES and SCHOOL
[S]ANATORIA.

2/6 a bottle
Plus bottle deposit 3d.
(returnable)

le

ng and palatable

Hunter. His daughter had contracted jaundice and he helped her convalesce by creating a glucose-rich drink flavoured with orange and lemon oils. Fortunately, the firm already had a mineral water factory and the drink was initially made and sold to hospitals as Glucozade, before being renamed Lucozade two years later.

The famous cellophane wrapper was Beecham's idea when it bought the recipe in 1938. It protected the drink from the degrading effects of light in much the same way as provincial haberdashers used to line their display windows with yellow cellophane to stop the cavalry twills and paisley silk dressing gowns being faded by the sun. Even today, the famous champagne house Roederer still wraps its Cristal champagne in the same way because the wine is bottled in colourless glass rather than green. Now there's a drink which really *does* aid recovery.

SOREEN MALT LOAF

Malt loaf is undeniably odd. If you baked a cake and it turned out like the dark squidgy malt loaf sold in supermarkets all over the country, you'd probably bin it and try a different recipe. This, of course, would be a mistake because it's supposed to look like that. The extraordinarily dense texture manages to be both sticky and rubbery – take one of those flip-flops made out of recycled tyres, leave it out in the hot sun all day and you'll get the general idea. Cutting neat slices is a complex skill that takes years of practice. OK, you can now buy pre-cut versions, but in our experience the slices just weld themselves together again after a day or two and you're back to square one.

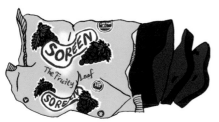

To toast or not to toast?

Having said all that, malt loaf is inexplicably delicious. It may look like an edible version of post-war utility furniture, but food bloggers devote hours of chat to the respective merits of eating it toasted or untoasted, with or without butter, chocolate or cheese. Don't any of these folk have day jobs?

The brand leader in the malt loaf world is Soreen, a company started by a family called Sorensen and currently owned by the family-owned Irish bakery business McCambridge. Presumably in an attempt to persuade young people to try it, Soreen market their 'Original Malt Loaf' as ninety-seven per cent fat free. But, as all wise virgins know, fat-free and low calorie are two very different things, and malt loaf is definitely not diet food. In fact, eat enough of it while drinking strong tea and sunbathing and the colour and texture of your thighs could soon come to bear a striking resemblance to the product.

BATTENBERG CAKE

Like Britain's Royal Family, Battenberg cake has a guilty and not-very-well-kept secret. It's German. Yet contrary to a scurrilous folk myth circulating on the Internet, it wasn't invented by Hitler's grandmother. In spite of its Germanic heritage, Battenberg remains right up there alongside teatime treats from every corner of this fair land – Bakewell Tarts, Eccles Cakes and Fondant Fancies. Just where is Fondant, exactly?

Marzipan and sympathy

Battenberg was the one cake guaranteed to lighten up the drabbest maiden aunt's tea table in the monochrome Britain of the 1950s and 60s. Apparently, Ernest Shackleton took a supply for energy on his arduous first and second Arctic expeditions. Mind you, if Shackleton really did lug along absolutely every British foodstuff that's been claimed, its really no wonder his dogs died in the attempt.

Like us Brits, Battenberg hides its true qualities behind a modest exterior. From the outside, it's harmless-looking, yellowish and emanates a faint whiff of almonds. Much like one of those maiden aunts, in fact. Yet slipped fresh out of its cellophane wrapping, it cuts into fat slabs like a dream. Only then is that Day-Glo chequerboard of melting pink and yellow sponge revealed in all its glory.

Don't glaze over, but here comes the history lesson. Each of the sponge quarters glued together with jam honours one of four Battenberg princes. The recipe was probably created in 1884, when one of the four princes, Prince Louis, got hitched to Queen Victoria's granddaughter, Princess Victoria of Hesse-Darmstadt.

Let's hope she liked marzipan. With Battenberg, there's no getting away from the stuff, as it makes up nearly a third of the entire shooting match. If you really don't like it, well you deserve sympathy – your only option is to try and swap yours with someone prepared to give up some of their pink and yellow squares.

A living legend

Today, consumption of many packet cakes may be falling, but Battenberg battles on. At the last count, the legendary if non-existent Mr Kipling is still knocking out a highly respectable 38 million Mini Battenbergs every year. But before he gets all the credit, we should mention it was J. Lyons and Company of Cadby Hall, Hammersmith, who popularized Battenberg in the 1930s. Maybe the firm's Continental founding families, the Salmons and the Glucksteins, remembered the cake from their youth and introduced it to the market. Either way, it soon became a top-selling line.

Battenberg cake also reminds us of the late authoress Barbara Cartland. She was pink, sickly sweet, and claimed to sell millions, but we have never met anyone who has actually bought anything written by her. Equally, we have never been in a supermarket and spotted anyone taking a Battenberg cake off a shelf and popping it into their shopping trolley. So do people buy them in secret from petrol stations, or just hide them under bags of rocket salad?

Battenberg is also one of those products that the popular press love to say is under 'threat'. As we write there seems to be is an imminent restriction on some artificial food colourings. Without these, it's said Battenberg would be no more. So what does it contain now? Well, reading one typical label, this is certainly not a cake for the intolerant. It packs in egg, milk, soya, wheat and nuts. Mysteriously, however, the one we bought already contains no artificial colours. Yet it's still bright pink and yellow. How do they do that?

Survivability	*8/10*
Trolley Embarrassment Factor	*7/10*
Versatility	*LOW*

READY BREK

It's hard to say why Ready Brek's 'central heating for kids' TV ads from the 70s turned out to be so memorable. It's not as if there was anything particularly clever about them: the kids ate up their bowls of Ready Brek and went off to school enveloped in a fuzzy orange glow of oaty warmth. But every time they appeared on their TV screens, Philippa and her brother would roll around on the sitting room carpet doubled up with laughter, for reasons which she now can't remember.

Of course there was something distinctly nuclear about the way those kids radiated, and in an era when rowdy CND rallies regularly made headlines, the jokes about Ready Brek were legion, particularly after the notorious partial meltdown at the Three Mile Island reactor in Pennsylvania in 1979.

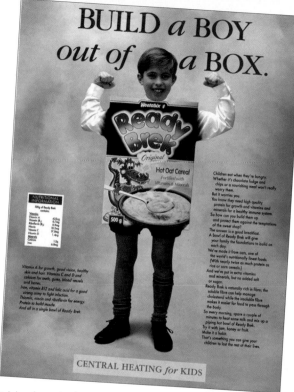

Eat your porridge

Quite why Ready Brek is still with us at all is a bit of a mystery too. Now that microwave ovens have done away with the horrible task of scouring a glutinous pan every time you fancy a bowl, making real porridge is short work.

Perhaps the truth is that Ready Brek is a kind of 'porridge-lite' for people who find the real thing a bit too, well, real and its gluey, wallpaper-paste texture bears little resemblance to anything your average hairy Celtic warrior might have called a hearty breakfast. And even though it's only made with rolled oats and wholegrain oat flour, it somehow tastes different to ordinary porridge too – but perhaps that's the added vitamins and minerals.

From hero to zero

Like so many other products, Ready Brek came about almost by accident. A factory manager in J. Lyons & Co's tea division began to experiment with a liquid derived from oat flakes and found that by drying it out he could turn it into a porridge substitute. The new 'instant porridge' was launched in 1957 and sales grew steadily for five years before petering out. Bewildered, the company commissioned a market research study and discovered to its surprise that traditional porridge eaters weren't buying Ready Brek: it was their children who were the big fans. Never slow to respond to customers, Lyons hastily relaunched their product as a children's cereal. By the mid-70s the range had been expanded and it soon became Britain's third most popular cereal.

Survivability	5/10
Trolley Embarrassment Factor	4/10
Versatility	LOW

Unfortunately it was also around this time that J. Lyons & Co ran into financial difficulties. Having risen from modest beginnings in the late 1800s to become the largest food manufacturing empire in Europe, by the early 1970s the company was financially overstretched and looking down the twin barrels of a recession and an oil crisis. Sky-high interest rates tipped the balance, and in 1978 Allied Breweries bought the company and, after a few years, began to sell off the various divisions. Weetabix snapped up Ready Brek in 1990 and nowadays, although it comes in three flavours (original, chocolate and honey), it's much the same as ever. The company has even brought back the glowing TV kids. If today's children find them as hilarious as Philippa used to please can they remind us why?

ATORA

Now it may be that the man who invented Atora suet just fancied a duvet day, or it may be that business was genuinely slack, but once upon a time in Manchester a French engraver named Gabriel Hugon found himself with nothing better to do than watch his wife laboriously chopping up a lump of beef suet. Unlikely as it may seem, this domestic vision proved to be his eureka moment, because it gave him a revolutionary idea: he would take the hassle out of cooking with suet by opening a chopped suet factory. Convinced that his idea was a bright one, the engraver did just that in 1893 and created one of the very first 'convenience foods'.

A load of bull

Modern cooks who've never had to prepare their own suet may be wondering what all the fuss was about. What they probably don't know is that long before you got to the chopping up stage, you first had to separate the beef fat from the meat and then clarify it by boiling it up with water. Next, it had to be left to cool so that it could re-solidify into purified fat, and only then could you finely chop it and actually use it to prepare a dish. Not exactly fast food, even by nineteenth century standards.

Fast it may not have been, but popular it certainly was. The first recorded mention of suet dates from 1617, when it was listed as one of the ingredients in Cambridge Pudding, a dessert regularly served at the university. By the end of the same century, suet crust began to be mentioned in cookbooks, and by Hugon's day, hearty suet pies, pastries, dumplings and puddings were regular fare for folk of all classes.

Hugon is said to have named his product after the Spanish word for bull: *toro* (though, being French, it seems more logical to suppose that he had the French word *toreau* in mind). Whichever it was, the man clearly had a thing about bulls because he also used teams of the beasts to haul his product around the country in painted wagons.

Jam-not-so-roly-poly

Hugon's factory prospered and surprisingly, given the collective phobia about eating 'fat' which has overtaken Britain in the past thirty years, Atora still produces about 2,300 tons of suet every year at it's factory in Cleveland. In the spirit of the age, however, some of it is now made from

not-so-roly-poly. But, in all honesty, we'd far rather have a smaller portion of the real thing – it's the perfect pudding to eat while watching Gillian McKeith on the telly. And on the subject of health, did you know that suet used to be recommended as a cough remedy? According to an old Atora cookbook, you simply add a teaspoonful to a glass of hot milk

vegetable rather than beef fat. The veggie version is also twenty-five per cent lower in fat than traditional beef suet, which provides some relief to those who prefer their jam-

at bedtime and no, you don't rub the noxious mixture on your chest, you drink it. Yuk! We're all for alternative medicines but there are limits.

Survivability	*5/10*
Trolley Embarrassment Factor	*2/10*
Versatility	*HIGH*

HEINZ SALAD CREAM

There's probably a scientific explanation as to why some foods we loved as kids taste strangely repellent to us as adults and Heinz Salad Cream is a fine example. As small children we both loaded it onto the floppy lettuce/tomato/cucumber/pickled beetroot combo that laughably passed as 'salad' back then, and if there was anything more delicious to blob onto cold, hard-boiled eggs we never discovered it. Today though, while Nigel still has the occasional yearning for the stuff, Philippa would rather douse her salad in diesel.

So when did Heinz salad cream begin to fall from grace? Like so many doomed love affairs, it's impossible to pinpoint the moment when the rot set in but it was probably one sunny day in the mid 1970s when Hellmann's Mayo sashayed onto the lunch table looking all St Tropez chic with its smart navy label. Overnight, salad cream suddenly looked a bit provincial and – worst sin of all in our teenage eyes – rather childish. Salad cream kept on showing up for a while, but nobody complained when mum quietly binned it.

British through and through

Which was a bit of a shame because while the bottled version may not be to everyone's taste, salad cream is a fine and thoroughly British institution. Those redoubtable Victorians Mrs Beeton and Eliza Acton both included recipes for it in their bestselling cookbooks, and it was clearly well-loved by the late 1800s. The bright boys at Heinz must have known this in 1925, because they plumped for salad cream when they were looking for a product to develop specifically for the British, rather than the US market. It took them eight years to perfect their version, in spite of the fact that both Beeton and Acton's recipes only listed about half a dozen ingredients. Heinz substituted vegetable oil for the fresh cream stipulated by both ladies although (tut tut) the company evidently didn't feel the need to change

the name accordingly. Nor did they ever get round to marketing the stuff in the US, which is why most Americans haven't a clue what salad cream is to this day.

Like SPAM, salad cream did rather nicely during the war years. Tomato ketchup may have disappeared, but in spite of being bombed – twice – the Heinz factory at Harlesden in Middlesex continued to bottle rivers of the stuff. People found it came in handy to pep up a variety of bland wartime foods and by the end of the war it was as much a staple in British larders as marmalade, mustard or pickled onions and remained so for more than thirty years.

Mayo schmayo

Inevitably, it was the aspirational 1980s that finally put the kybosh on salad cream. In an era when upwardly mobile yuppies yearned to pass themselves off as urban sophisticates or green-wellied Sloanes, there was no place for it. Mayonnaise was what the movers and shakers ate in their deli sandwiches across the pond. Mayonnaise was what yacht-owning millionaires expected to see on their lobster salad when they popped over to Antibes. Salad cream was what your gran put on her tea table: too naff for words.

It was finally around the millennium when Heinz loudly suggested that its salad cream might be withdrawn from the British market. A cynical ploy possibly, but it produced the required blaze of publicity, including a clutch of B-list celebrities telling us how they couldn't live without the stuff. Within weeks Heinz had to 'save' the product, although it didn't go unnoticed that the price seemed to have mysteriously risen at the checkout.

Mixed with a little tomato ketchup and dolloped over prawns and chopped lettuce, Heinz Salad Cream is a key component of that retro seaside hotel favourite prawn cocktail. Perhaps that's one of the reasons it has retained enough fans to stay on the supermarket shelves. As for your authors, Nigel still swears that nothing beats a ready salted crisp-and-salad-cream sandwich on sliced white. Some people will eat anything.

SPAM

Some foods have such delicious names that the merest mention of them makes your taste buds tingle: syllabub; asparagus; bouillabaisse ... who could resist them? SPAM is less fortunate. Was a more slab-sided and unappealing word ever invented to describe something we're supposed to eat? Ken Daigneau is the culprit. He won a competition to name Hormel Foods' new product in 1936 and trousered $100 for his trouble. Why SPAM? Well, some people believe that the word comes from 'spiced ham'; others argue that it must be an acronym because the letters are always printed in upper case; there are many other suggestions but most of them are not so much unpalatable as unprintable ...

Miracle meat

SPAM began life in the Great Depression of the 1930s when Jay C. Hormel came up with a recipe involving ham, pork, sugar, salt, water and potato starch for his father's food factory in Austin, Minnesota. After a little more thought, he added sodium nitrite to stop his pink meaty concoction turning grey, which was undoubtedly a smart move. Even so, SPAM didn't really take off until Hormel began advertising it as 'Miracle Meat'. Soon, the Austin factory was turning it out by the pallet-load, and a few years later, another global disaster turned it into an international superstar: the Second World War. Unlike beef, Hormel's miracle meat was never rationed and quickly became a staple source of cheap, long-lasting protein. US troops

"SPAM"

● **"SPAM"** distinguishes a special product made from pure pork shoulder-meat, with ham meat added.

● **"SPAM"** is sold only in 12-oz. tins.

● **"SPAM"** is a registered Trade Mark, and can be used only in respect of the product of Geo. A. Hormel & Co., Austin, Minnesota, U.S.A.

● **"SPAM"** will be for sale as soon as we can manage it.

stationed in the Pacific ate it for breakfast, lunch and dinner, and handed it out to the locals everywhere they went. Presumably they were sick of the sight of it.

That's why the residents of Hawaii, Guam and the Commonwealth of the Northern Mariana Islands still eat more SPAM than almost anyone else – an average of sixteen cans per head per year. It's apparently so popular, even the local McDonald's and Burger King outlets feature SPAM dishes on their menus. Let's just hope they don't put it in the shakes. Combined with local ingredients such as rice and seaweed, SPAM has grown to be an iconic part of the islands' culinary heritage. Every grocery store sells it and, for communities where poverty is widespread, it's cheap. Talking of which, seventy years on, another global credit crunch seems to be giving

SPAM a boost. Putting fresh meat on the table every day has become so expensive for hard-pressed Americans that many are turning to SPAM to fill the gap. Production has been at full stretch at the Hormel Foods plant in Austin, and far from laying people off, the management has even been getting staff to work overtime.

Spam, Spam, marvellous Spam

For us Brits, SPAM was another of those products that arrived with the US army. Thanks to rationing, it filled a hole in our diets and SPAM fritters even replaced scarce fish at the chippie. Unfortunately, long after the war was over, it remained the friend of lazy school cooks everywhere and a whole generation grew up to believe they should never have to eat it again.

Nearly 7 billion cans of SPAM have been sold worldwide since 1936 and, inevitably, it now comes in a range of flavours. Depending on where you live, you may be able to buy such treats as SPAM with cheese, or bacon, a lite or hot & spicy version, or even SPAM spread. Not that there's any hurry to eat it once it's in the cupboard because, as the Hormel website

neatly puts it: 'It's like meat with a pause button'. We can't possibly leave this subject without mentioning that Monty Python routine about the café full of singing Vikings, where every dish on the menu involved SPAM. It's been suggested that the endless SPAM song is the reason why repetitive and annoying junk email came to be called 'spam'. The Python connection took an even stranger turn in 2006, when a limited edition 'Stinky French Garlic SPAM' was launched to cash-in on the West End opening of the hit musical Spamalot. The variety paid homage to a celebrated scene where King Arthur and his knights trade colourful insults with a bunch of French soldiers. Not that the show's creator Eric Idle touches the stuff; he's a vegetarian nowadays and once described SPAM as looking 'like sliced flesh'. That's one celebrity endorsement which probably won't make it into the next advertising campaign.

Survivability	*9/10*
Trolley Embarrassment Factor	*10/10*
Versatility	*HIGH*

NEAPOLITAN ICE CREAM

Svelte in its cardboard sleeve, Neapolitan ice cream was always classier than its soft scoop, plastic-tub rivals. Pretty and chic, it smelt of beach cafés on the Costa del Sol, where the ice cream came in heavy tall-stemmed frosted glass dishes on little white saucers. Even at home, it was always a special moment when we peeled open the packet and watched mum wield a ruler to make sure there was no sibling wrangling about who got the biggest helping.

Sunday sundae

Neapolitan may have originated in Naples but neither of us has ever seen it in Italy. Food historians will tell you the term covers any collection of flavours pressed together into a mould or block, and nineteenth-century European recipe books often mention pistachio, chocolate and cherry. But it was in America that the commercial ice cream market really took off with the arrival of motorized delivery vehicles. Soon, families were whiling away their Sundays in ice cream parlours and the more strait-laced churches were muttering darkly about the 'sinfulness' of rich ice cream sodas on the Sabbath. Quick-thinking soda jerks smartly took the heat out of the situation by whipping up a more restrained ice cream 'Sunday' (as it was originally known) for their customers instead.

Here in Britain, it was wartime and in 1942 the government banned ice cream manufacture outright due to milk shortages. According to the *New York Times*, aggrieved US airmen got round the problem by stowing cans of ice cream mix in the tail gunner's cockpit in their B-29s. Apparently, the combination of freezing air and engine vibration produced a very acceptable result. It seems Americans just can't manage without their Neapolitan; NASA astronauts even took a freeze-dried version into space – the chunks are re-hydrated with saliva in the

Survivability	*6/10*
Trolley Embarrassment Factor	*7/10*
Versatility	*LOW*

mouth – dee-licious. Hiking and novelty shops stock the stuff if you're curious to know what it tastes like.

Blame it on Mrs T

Talking of food atrocities, it was British scientists who came up with the idea for 'soft scoop'. Bizarrely, one of young chemistry graduate Margaret Thatcher's earliest jobs was to research ways to 'inflate' ice cream by forcing air into it. Dopey consumers lapped it up because it was easier to serve than old-fashioned block-type ice creams like Neapolitan. It took us twenty years to realize that whipped up chemicals and air are no substitute for real ice cream and about twenty seconds

Whoopee! New Wall's Harlequin
ice cream in fancy dress

Dress up a meal with Harlequin today •
Craziest ice cream you ever tasted •
Checks of Strawberry, Chocolate, Vanilla •
One of seven Wall's 2/6 Family Sweets •

Wall's Harlequin

Wall's have all the FUN FLAVOURS!

for ice cream executives to start charging us a 'premium' price for what used to be considered ordinary ice cream.

Today, Brits don't rank highly when it comes to troughing down ice cream. At nine litres per head per year we don't even make it into the top ten ice-cream-eating countries, although the sweet-toothed Scots are doing their best to change that. Vanilla remains our favourite flavour, and cardboard-packaged Neapolitan has virtually disappeared, although it's widely available in plastic tubs. You can even opt for a non-dairy version – but isn't that a contradiction in terms?

COLMAN'S MUSTARD

When asked how on earth he had managed to turn a humble condiment into a money-spinner, Jeremiah Colman said that he made his money from the mustard people left on the side of their plates.

Think of English Mustard, and you think of Colman's. It was in 1814 when miller Jeremiah Colman first advertised his mustard in the Norwich Chronicle, after his family took over Stoke Mill just south of the City. The mill still stands to this day and is now a restaurant. The long history of the family business is closely tied to that of Norwich itself. The bull's head logo first appeared in 1855, with the familiar red and yellow livery added to the label in 1866, the year Colman's got its Royal Warrant from Queen Victoria. Colman's moved to its present works at Carrow in 1856, where it was a pioneer of social welfare, employing a factory nurse and opening a school for employees' children.

Keen as …

In 1903, Colman's bought out the London mustard makers, Keen & Sons, who supplied the city's chophouses. Keen & Sons are widely thought to have inspired the saying 'as keen as mustard', but the phrase had actually been in print long before Keen came on the scene. However there doesn't seem to be any convincing explanation for the origin of that other well-worn phrase 'to cut the mustard', as an indicator of competence or top quality. Mustard seeds and plants are tough to cut with knives, and mustard is cut, or diluted, with vinegar to make it more palatable, but that's about as far as it goes.

Mustard was mentioned in the Bible, and the grainy version really has been around since the year dot. Here in Britain, in 1720, a Mrs Clements is credited with being the first to mill and sieve the seeds to produce a creamier product. Colman's uses a mixture of brown and white mustard seeds, adding wheat flour for texture and turmeric for colour. English mustard is fiery and pungent, perfect with cold meats and strong cheese. The French are also no slouches when it comes to mustard, and in Dijon they've been making it for centuries, using only brown seeds and dousing them in vinegar to temper the heat.

English or French?

The question of when it's acceptable to choose a milder French mustard has been a matter of long-running culinary debate, and the cookery writer Elizabeth David wrote that her own interest was awakened when she heard what the renowned London restaurateur Marcel Boulestin had to say about a waiter who offered him the wrong sort back in the 1930s: 'He offers us English mustard with the entrecôte? He must go!'

One influential public figure who wasn't content with either is the Italian-born England football manager Fabio Capello. He reportedly took ketchup, mustard and mayonnaise off the players' dining table and replaced them with what he called 'the fresh sauces of the Mediterranean diet'. It seems reasonable to conclude that whatever kinds of promotion the current brand owner Unilever goes in for in future, we won't be seeing this most English of brands displayed on the shirt-fronts of our national team.

Survivability	*10/10*
Trolley Embarrassment Factor	*0/10*
Versatility	*HIGH*

Mince with a surprise

Mmm . . . Ooh . . . Ah ! Doesn't it smell good? Tastes good too! It's mince, served the new Bisto way! Get the Bisto Recipe Book. It opens your eyes to lots of surprise " twists " that turn family favourites into smash hits ! Write for your free copy to Cerebos Ltd., Dept. RB., Willesden, N.W.10.

SEND NOW FOR FREE BISTO RECIPE BOOK !

Ah!

BISTO

makes the meal !

BISTO

We've tried to avoid any petty elements of class distinction creeping into these pages, but when it comes to gravy there's just no getting away from it: posh people like thin gravy – often little more than pan juices whisked up with a drop of yesterday's claret and a little butter and flour to add body if you're lucky. The rest of us prefer our gravy thicker and all but threatening to drown the meat and two veg. When it comes to Sunday lunch, nothing is more divisive than what people pour over their roast beef and Yorkshire pudding.

Bisto gravy powder was invented in 1908 by two men named Roberts and Patterson. They worked together at the Cerebos salt factory in Cheshire, and the story goes that their wives challenged them to produce something to help them make smooth gravy more easily. Experiments mixing starch, caramel, yeast, vegetable powders and salt eventually produced the original Bisto many may remember in its tall, thin box. A new business was born, with brown hairnets for people working on the gravy side of the plant and white for those working on salt.

Ah! Bisto

Bisto is said to be short for 'Browns, Seasons and Thickens in One'. It isn't; it was just a made up name, which explains why the 'i' in Bisto doesn't fit the slogan. The big change for Bisto came in 1979, with the introduction of complete gravy granules that could simply be mixed up with boiling water rather than meat juices. The granules were a true innovation – producing a smooth, aromatic and surprisingly delicate gravy – and soon the company was cannibalizing the sales of its old powdered Bisto and dominating the market, which it does to this day.

Those pastry kids

Bisto has always boosted its appeal through clever advertising – positioning the brand as part of the family. The ragamuffin Bisto Kids, created by cartoonist Wilf Owen, made their first appearance as early as 1919, catching a whiff of the cooking smells and sighing, 'Ah! Bisto'. While the cartoon kids no longer feature, Bisto's owners have been praised for their ongoing 'Ah! Nights' campaign. It cleverly builds on recent research findings that crime, teenage pregnancy, truancy, poor academic performance and the rest have a lot to do with family dysfunction, and encourages families to sit round a table one night a week and eat 'proper' food together.

Unfortunately for Bisto, the more our culinary horizons have expanded, the fewer meals we seem to eat involving traditional gravy.

One feisty couple that we know fought like cat and dog over preferred gravy thickness. Many a gravy boat must have come to grief in the conflict. Détente wasn't reached until their children were old enough to take sides in the regular Sunday lunchtime battle. The partner with a preference for pan juices was eventually obliged to concede victory to the thick gravy brigade at the other end of the table. Another triumph for Bisto.

Survivability	*8/10*
Trolley Embarrassment Factor	*7/10*
Versatility	*LOW*

SUN-PAT PEANUT BUTTER

Arachibutyrophobics, be very afraid. Believe it or not, that's the term for the fear of peanut butter sticking to the roof of your mouth. The rest of us love our peanut butter – simultaneously nutty and buttery (although contains no butter), sweet and salty. No need to chew, it just hangs out in your mouth, getting to know you.

Peanut butter came to Britain with the US forces. That may be why one friend's gran wouldn't have it in the house because it was 'too Yankee'. Smooth is favoured on the US east coast; crunchy on the west. They all look like the contents of a baby's nappy.

A legendary sandwich

Doctors recommended protein-rich peanut paste for patients with bad teeth, and it was Joseph L. Rosefield who stopped the peanut oil separating and created America's

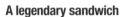

Sun-pat has more protein than chicken, turkey or beef. Shhh!

famous 'Skippy' brand. Elvis Presley especially loved fried bread filled with peanut butter, bananas and bacon. Surprising he even made it to forty-two, really.

Sun-Pat was born in 1960 in the Derbyshire town of Hadfield. Renamed Royston Veysey, it was where the oddball TV comedy *League of Gentlemen* was filmed. Imported peanuts are roasted; sugar, salt and stabilizer is added and the whole lot is ground up and popped into jars. It's said to be a good standby if you run out of shaving foam and it cleans shoes up a treat. You can also use it for getting chewing gum out of your hair but neither of us was willing to test this. Apparently it sticks to your palate because of the hydration of the protein, which draws moisture out of your mouth. Try adding something wet – like jam, mashed banana, honey, or – wait for it – Nutella. You might think that would be even more nuts and you'd be right.

MARMITE

A few years ago the people who make Marmite calculated that they were selling enough of the stuff for every man, woman and child in Britain to eat one hundred Marmite soldiers every year. Setting aside the delicate psychology of why grown men and women should still be eating toast soldiers of any description, that really is an awful lot of Marmite. And when you remember the millions who would vigorously lick the carpet in their local pub rather than allow Marmite anywhere near their taste buds, it makes you wonder just how many jars some fans are getting through.

Don't mention the war

It's over a hundred years since The Marmite Food Extract Company in Burton-upon-Trent came up with the idea of turning used yeast from the local Bass Brewery into a savoury spread. And that's all it is, spare brewery yeast, with added vitamins, vegetable and spice extracts to improve the flavour. Delicious or disgusting depending on your point of view, the tar-like substance with its distinctive mushroomy aroma and dinky yellow-lidded jar has enjoyed iconic status for decades.

As for the name, Marmite was originally sold in the small

Life is fun when you're pretty and young — so much fun there's hardly time to eat. But do start the day with a nourishing breakfast. There may not be time to cook — but there *is* time for Marmite on toast. Savoury flavour and B$_2$ vitamins on toast!

MARMITE
on toast... mm tasty!

Boys and Girls
come in from play

Tʜᴇʏ'ᴠᴇ ʙᴇᴇɴ ᴏᴜᴛ all after-noon. Stalking Red Indians, hunting a tiger in the garden. Now they're ravenous. Ready for a good big tea. Ready for delicious Marmite sandwiches. They're appetising, and made in a moment. It's good to know that Marmite does the family so much good. It contains essential B₂ vitamins.

MARMITE
the finest "spread" on toast or bread

earthenware dish still pictured on the front of the pot, which in France is known as a marmite. History doesn't relate why a company based in the brewing capital of Great Britain would want to give its new product a French name. The glass jars we all know and love were introduced in the 1920s and since then there's been no escaping this oddest of foods.

Fans are peculiarly possessive about their Marmite. Some are still incandescent about the effrontery of the present brand owners, Unilever, in daring to sell it in squeezable plastic pots. They'd far rather stick to buying Marmite in its traditional stumpy glass jar, even if it does mean digging through that disquieting layer of other people's toast crumbs. Talking of toast, the perfect way to spread Marmite is so hotly contested that the publication of a single letter on the subject in the *Independent* newspaper a couple of years ago gave rise to sack loads of correspondence and an avalanche of argumentative emails from impassioned fans.

But Marmite might also have a role to play in alleviating conflict if the original thinker Edward de Bono is to be believed. In a talk to Foreign Office officials, he pointed out that communities that eat unleavened bread are known to experience heightened levels of aggression due to zinc deficiency, and ventured that Marmite might be just the thing to bring down the diplomatic temperature in the Arab-Israeli conflict. It's an intriguing theory, but given the fervent 'love it or loath it' factionalism the stuff stirs up amongst even mild-mannered British breakfasters, we shudder to think of the consequences had Whitehall mandarins summoned up the energy to act on his advice.

Bear-faced cheats

At least nutritionists agree that Marmite is a good source of B vitamins, and the Vegetarian Society even suggested mixing it with vegetable protein and feeding it to your

dog. Even poor old Paddington Bear was forced to forego his traditional marmalade sandwiches and take to cheese and Marmite instead as part of the 'Squeezable' launch. Animal cruelty? You might think so, we couldn't possibly comment.

Oh, and in case you're wondering, Vegemite is very similar to Marmite in that it's also a dark brown paste made from yeast extract. BUT IT'S NOT THE SAME. Admittedly, it's a national food in Australia, yet its American owners Kraft Foods have signally failed to build a fan base for it anywhere else, including the US. Draw your own conclusions.

Survivability	*10/10*
Trolley Embarrassment Factor	*0/10*
Versatility	*MEDIUM*

BIRD'S CUSTARD

They say a true Englishman has custard running through his veins. Whether this is the sticky powdered variety created by the famous Mr Bird, or 'proper' custard, made from cream, sugar, eggs and vanilla pods, is unclear.

'What do you want on your crumble?'

What is beyond doubt is that Bird's Custard ran through our childhoods like an unctuous yellow river. We drowned rhubarb or apricot crumbles and steamed puddings in it. We deluged sliced bananas and tinned yellow cling peaches. We even poured it cold over leftover cake soaked in fruit and jelly, topped it with cream and called it trifle.

As his shop sign in Bell Street, Birmingham proudly

Survivability	7/10
Trolley Embarrassment Factor	5/10
Versatility	MEDIUM

proclaimed, Alfred Bird was an experimental chemist. His wife loved custard, but was allergic to eggs. In 1837, Bird solved this very twenty-first-century sounding dietary problem by creating an egg-less, powdered substitute that thickened up nicely when heated up with milk and sugar. Later, Bird went into production, widely advertising his wholesome new convenience food. The company headquarters in Digbeth was once one of Birmingham's best-known landmarks, and locals will tell you that the windows were always dusted with yellow custard powder.

The comeback kid

Bird wasn't the only custard baron around. There was Brown & Polson, Pearce Duff and Cremola. Another was a family company in Clerkenwell, London, called Monk & Glass – eventually chaired by the late comedian Bob Monkhouse's father. Custard clearly didn't run through Bob's veins. As he himself once put it: 'When I said I was going to become a comedian, they all laughed. Well, they're not laughing now.'

-"And some have greatness thrust upon them."

BIRD'S CUSTARD makes children sturdy!

By the 1980s, custard had passed its sell-by date. We blame school dinner-ladies – they made it with too much water and left powdery lumps that took the enamel off your teeth. Then came the even leaner 1990s, when pudding was usually stewed fruit mixed with sharp-tasting yogurt, topped with a layer of gravel.

Today, custard is quite the comeback kid. Ready-made versions with fresher ingredients have raised the bar, providing higher quality lubrication for modern classics like sticky toffee pudding. To be frank, the amazing success of an industrial product so unlike the real thing remains one of the mysteries of grocery retailing. As one real custard fan once memorably put it, the packet variety is the kind of food the British have always done best: created through advertising, dripping with cultural baggage, yet devoid of nutritional value. Seconds, anyone?

FRENCH FANCIES

Why 'French' Fancies? Well, perhaps it's because these vibrant little sponge cakes nestling in their frilly paper cases do rather bring to mind naughty can-can girls in white frilly knickers. The pastel-coloured icing and the delightfully bijou smallness of them is utterly boudoir-ish, but where the French connection truly lies remains a mystery.

An elegant sufficiency

There is, of course, a good reason why French Fancies have remained so petite in an era when so many packaged foods

are growing, Alice in Wonderland-like, before our very eyes: they're sweet – so sweet, in fact, that it's virtually impossible to eat more than one at a sitting unless you're under

the age of ten. Even devoted admirers commonly use the word 'sickly' to describe these vanilla-cream-topped sponge cubes wrapped in fondant icing, and admit that one French Fancy is generally more than a sufficiency. Nonetheless, much has also been written about the fact that because each box contains eight rather than nine cakes you only get two cakes rather than three in each of the colours. Are you following this? And does it really matter? Apparently it does, particularly if you like lemon icing more than strawberry or chocolate. One solution we found is to eat them blindfolded, because we think its only possible to reliably identify the yellow ones.

Exceedingly dull cakes

Own-brand versions notwithstanding, Mr Kipling's is still the most popular brand of French Fancy, and rightly so, since its parent company Rank Hovis McDougall (RHM) invented both of them. It was the mid-1960s, a time when the stigma attached to 'shop bought' as opposed to 'home-made' cake was disappearing as more women woke up to the fact that giving up baking didn't automatically make them bad wives or mothers. Unfortunately, the range of cakes on offer was pretty dull; the supermarkets were starting to see off local bakeries, but the cakes they stocked were a far cry from those of today. RHM decided there was money to be made and set to work on a new range of colourfully packaged cakes. Two years later, the job was done and the fictitious Mr Kipling was invented, along with the tag line 'exceedingly good cakes', to promote the new collection. Rather surprisingly in the youth-obsessed, zoned-out zeitgeist of the swinging 60s, the nation immediately took the cheery, avuncular and unashamedly old-fashioned Mr K to their hearts. Within twelve months, nine out of ten of us knew who he was, and by 1976 Mr Kipling had become the leading UK cake brand.

French Fancies were one of the original twenty-strong line-up of Mr Kipling cakes, along with Battenberg, Almond Slices and Manor House Cake, all of which are still in production. Today we spend more than £1.2 billion pounds on such packaged cakes every year and Mr Kipling is still numero uno, bringing in about £200m a year for its owner.

They tell us that the non-existent Mr Kipling is particularly partial to a Cherry Bakewell. He's not alone, 220,000 of them are eaten every day. But for those for whom the French Fancy remains queen of the cakewalk, 2008 really was a year to celebrate. That was when the Big French Fancy was launched – a giant version of the original little cake. Frankly, it looks to us like something that might chase you down the road in an LSD-induced hallucination, but if it sounds like the answer to your childhood prayers, just remember: never eat anything bigger than your head (well, not in one go).

McVITIE'S JAFFA CAKES

Jaffa Cakes have been handed what must be the ultimate seal of approval in the cake and biscuit world. After vigorous argument between some of the world's most prestigious lexicographers, the term 'Jaffa Cake' has made its first appearance in the *Oxford English Dictionary*. It's an honour shared with the Custard Cream, but one that has yet to be handed to the Club Biscuit, or the Penguin. The definition for Jaffa Cake is certainly workmanlike, though it perhaps fails to capture the pleasure of eating one: it's just 'a sponge biscuit with an orange-flavoured jelly filling and chocolate topping'. Apparently it's in because the term has diversified into use as a nickname, is often mentioned in novels and is associated with – wait for it – a small sub-culture in bondage sex. No, we're not sure what that's all about either, better ask those weirdo lexicographers.

750 million and counting

The Jaffa Cake is one of those edibles where the whole is more pleasing than its components. Jaffa Cakes also invite ritual eating – biting round the edge to reveal the smashing orangey bit in the middle, then prising or licking off the chocolate so you can carefully detach the jelly, which you eat at the end as a treat after demolishing the spongy bit. Repeat this procedure until queasy, or the packet is empty.

The brand leader McVitie's says over 750 million of its Jaffa Cakes are scoffed every year, which is apparently enough to reach from London to Australia and back, if you laid them end-to-end. (Why do they always say that? Technically it would be far easier to lay them sideways, straight out of the packet. Only then they'd probably only reach Cairo ...)

These days, Jaffa Cakes are made in Manchester, though

Survivability	*9/10*
Trolley Embarrassment Factor	*4/10*
Versatility	*LOW*

they were first created over seventy years ago at a McVitie's bakery in Edinburgh. So who actually came up with the idea? Well, McVitie's itself doesn't know – it says it has no records from the time. All we do know is that the late actor Ian Richardson, who played scheming politician Francis Urquhart in the TV drama *House of Cards*, once claimed his father was the inventor. It's certainly plausible – he was apparently works manager at the factory. Frustratingly, the company insists it can neither confirm nor deny this claim. It's all uncannily reminiscent of Urquhart's own signature phrase: 'You might think that; I couldn't possibly comment'.

Any friend of Vatman ...

One idea was to call them Jaffa Bakes. Whatever they had been named, it probably wouldn't have prevented all the trouble when McVitie's famously went up against HM Customs and Excise to prove that its product was a cake and not a biscuit – and therefore not a 'luxury' and subject to Value Added Tax. McVitie's masterstroke was to bake a giant Jaffa Cake for the hearing's chairman, saying that if it was demonstrably a cake, then so were its normal small versions in the packets. This argument won the day, successfully establishing a distinction between cakes and biscuits, another being that biscuits go soft when stale, whilst cakes go hard. The precedent also helped Marks & Spencer some years later when it had a run-in with the revenue over chocolate teacakes. The government's loss of the Jaffa case has already cost the UK economy a reported £30 million in lost tax revenue. Pretty small

beer compared to the cost of refinancing the UK banking sector after the credit crunch, but you rarely see a Jaffa Cake on a civil service tea tray.

Mind you, while the precise nature of a Jaffa Cake was important to lawyers and the taxman, does anyone else actually care if it's a biscuit or a cake? You certainly don't if you are thirteen years old, home from school and hungry. Incredibly, a survey into family eating habits found that one in ten parents thought Jaffa Cakes, chips and cola drinks counted towards a child's five-a-day tally of fruit and vegetables.

These days, Jaffa Cakes are multiplying. There are bars and muffins and mini-rolls, plus non-orangey fillings like berry, apple and blackcurrant. They're also on offer in strange pods and individually packaged 'snack packs', which we find mildly depressing, like receiving beautifully wrapped carpet slippers for Christmas. But there's no knocking the original Jaffa Cakes, especially as they contain only forty-eight calories and one gram of fat. That's one biscuit, sadly, not the whole packet.

CORNED BEEF

If you find it hard to fight your way into a can of corned beef now, think how much trickier it was in the early days of meat canning, when the opening instructions on tins involved the use of a hammer and chisel. Tins with their own key opener first went on sale in 1866 and have been lacerating the fingers of infuriated (and hungry) corned-beef fans ever since.

Living dangerously

Six years ago the dangers were even raised in the House of Lords, when the Government of the day was asked to encourage the food industry to redesign them. Their noble lords thoroughly chewed over the dangers posed by both the traditional key-opener cans and the more recent but equally lethal ring-pull variety. During the debate it emerged officials had done 'much work' on the cans, encouraging manufacturers to adopt a special coating to make it easier to extract the contents. As a result, they noted triumphantly, the number of accidents caused by corned beef cans had fallen dramatically

to just over three thousand a year. Three thousand? Three thousand? Surely, if any other foodstuff was responsible for carnage on that scale it would have been outlawed years ago.

No government, of course, would dare to suggest such a thing, because the truth is that we Brits adore the stuff. Some fans have even made a pilgrimage to the site of the vast former Fray Bentos factory in Uruguay that churned out tinned corned beef for over a century until it closed in 1979 and recently became a museum. Once there, and doubtless to the bewilderment of the tour guide, they often become emotional at the teatime memories the place name evokes. Even Prince Charles, who visited in 1999, commented with feeling that he had childhood memories of eating Fray Bentos

Survivability	**8/10**
Trolley Embarrassment Factor	**6/10**
Versatility	**MEDIUM**

corned beef 'until it came out of his ears'. The comment must have surprised newspaper readers just over the border in Argentina, where housewives apparently only buy corned beef as dog food.

Bully for you

Although it has traditionally been made in South America, corned beef has a long and honourable heritage over here. 'Bully beef', as it was known, is beef preserved by curing it in brine and then boiling it, and was central to army rations, not least because it could be eaten cold, straight from the can. The name was filched from the French *bouilli* or boiled beef, which the French army was given in the Franco-Prussian war.

Corned beef is not, however, without its detractors. With that much fat and salt not even its best friend could honestly claim that it's good for you, and neither does it have a flawless health record. In 1964, more than five hundred people were admitted to hospital with typhoid after a six pound can of Argentinian corned beef contaminated a slicing machine at a William Low supermarket in Aberdeen's West End. An investigation showed that during processing the can had been cooled in untreated river water and the organism had found its way in through a hole in the seam. It was one of the worst food poisoning incidents of the twentieth century; some patients had to spend three months in hospital, and 25,000 holiday-makers cancelled their trips. All of which, it later emerged, could have been avoided. Four outbreaks associated with Argentinian corned beef had already been recorded in the previous year and the UK had sent out a chief agricultural inspector to find out what was going on. In spite of having found the cause, he'd chosen not to recall two corned beef shipments already being distributed in the UK. A month later, meat from the suspect batch found its way to Aberdeen.

Although corned beef is most widely used as a sandwich filling, corned beef hash surely deserves an honourable mention. Derived from the French word *hacher* meaning to chop, fried 'hash' became common in England in the mid-seventeenth century, and by the early 1900s 'hash houses' (no, not what you're thinking) or 'diners' were commonly serving it. Americans reckon hash tastes better with a fried egg on top and, of course, they're perfectly entitled to their opinion. Then again, the pickled brisket that passes for corned beef in the US is very different to our own, as indeed are the two varieties of corned beef sold in Germany. Holiday-makers you have been warned: just pop a couple of tins of Fray Bentos in your suitcase and you'll be fine.

HEINZ TOMATO KETCHUP

Ask for some ketchup anywhere (do not do this on any account if Marco Pierre White is cooking your meal) and it's a dead cert you'll end up with tomato. But there was a time when you might have been offered a savoury dash of mushroom, anchovy or even lobster ketchup.

The word 'ketchup' probably comes from the Chinese *ke-tsiap*, a tangy pickled fish condiment that originates in Asia. Sailors brought liquid ketchup to England, where its character altered as home-grown flavourings – such as nuts, shallots, cucumber and lemon peel – were added.

You say tomayto

The killer ketchup ingredient – tomato – seems to have made its first appearance in print in an American recipe of 1801. The first man to sell it stateside was Jonas Yerkes. His raw materials weren't promising – little more than the slops left from the tomato canning process, which he boiled into a thin tomato sauce, using plenty of sugar and some vinegar. Other makers followed suit,

but those early products weren't up to much. Sometimes the tomatoes were rotten or the ketchup was packed with unsuitable fillers. We worry about additives now, but at that time coal tar was used as a colouring, and nasty preservatives such as sodium benzoate were added – all of which sometimes made people ill and gave the product a bad reputation.

So you might say it was a brave Henry John Heinz who chose tomato ketchup as one of his first new products when relaunching his family food company in Pittsburgh after bankruptcy. Fortunately, the market turned out to be as ripe as the juicy red fruit selected by his brewers. For a start, his tomatoes contained more pectin, giving his ketchup body. He added spices and much more sugar, vinegar and salt, which improved the taste

Survivability	*10/10*
Trolley Embarrassment Factor	*1/10*
Versatility	*MEDIUM*

and did away with the need for those dodgy preservatives. He also chose glass bottles, so his customers could see his ketchup was pure and not packed out with cheap bits of turnip. Word spread, and in 1886, Fortnum's in London bought five cases. By 1946, when the first British factory was opened near Wigan, Heinz Tomato Ketchup was a household name, and now sales top £100 million in Britain alone.

A new kind of taste

Entirely accidentally, Heinz had also stumbled on a fifth human taste. Alongside sour, sweet, salty and bitter, 'unami' was first identified by Japanese physics professor Kidunae Ikeda. It best translates as 'savoury' or 'deliciousness', and it is the essence of the flavour-enhancer monosodium glutamate. Luckily for Heinz, such glutamates occur naturally in foods such as cooked tomatoes, mushrooms and soy sauce. Some people also like to bang on about the benefits of the antioxidant lycopene, associated with decreased cancer risk. But that seems a bit

rich if you are slathering your ketchup over a fatty meal.

The advent of squeezable upside-down bottles has perhaps been a step too far for ketchup traditionalists, but they are designed to overcome the reluctance of the sauce to emerge from the neck of the bottle at any speed faster than a recorded 0.028 mph (if it flows much faster, apparently, the batch is rejected). And while we're blinding you with science, it may also be worth mentioning that ketchup is technically a pseudo-plastic, sharing properties with blood, whipped cream and nail polish. Experts say you can ease it out of a glass bottle by tapping it on the neck with two fingers. This applies a force that temporarily reduces the viscosity and gets it dolloping onto your plate. If only someone had told Nigel that as a child. Out to tea with a friend, he was traumatized by the shame of shaking a reluctant ketchup bottle, only to see its contents shoot out all over his friend's mum's dining room. As the old rhyme goes: 'Careful with the ketchup bottle, none'll come and then a lot'll'!

VESTA PACKET MEALS

It came as a shock to discover Vesta Curry, Paella, Risotto and Chow Mein still lurking on the shelves of a local store. And no – they hadn't just been sitting there gathering dust since the mid 1960s. Rediscovering those fry-and-simmer meal kits of dehydrated sauce and rice or noodles lurches us back to the time when the contents of those packets provided welcome relief from our more usual meals of grey meat and two vegetables and mince swimming in thin gravy.

Vesta meals made their first appearance in 1962 and boomed in the 1970s – becoming a staple of student larders. The fact that Vesta Curry, with its seven per cent of freeze-dried, 'chopped and shaped beef', didn't taste like any real dish ever served on the Indian subcontinent was beside the point – the truth was that some of us had yet to set foot inside an Indian or Chinese restaurant. Mass long-haul travel had not taken off, so we had nothing to compare it to.

Just add water

Vesta meals at least offered us some stronger tastes at a time when only ardent cooks kept anything more exotic than dried parsley in their kitchen cupboards. The spicing in the mixtures woke up our taste buds when they hit the pan. Before Vesta, whoever heard of putting sultanas in a savoury dish, or emptying a mysterious silver sachet of salty soy sauce over your freshly fried crispy noodles? (Why was it, by the way, that at least two of the noodles refused to cook, and then went black?) Visiting Chinese restaurants later, it was a real disappointment to discover they rarely served crispy noodles.

Vesta's masterstroke was to spot that the snobbish, dinner

Survivability	1/10
Trolley Embarrassment Factor	10/10
Versatility	LOW

party cuisine of TV's Fanny Craddock and women's magazines put most ordinary people off cooking anything remotely unfamiliar. Unlike experimenting

with a recipe, the result with a Vesta meal kit was just the same every time. Men could even be trusted to rip open the various packets and follow the step-by-step instructions. A whole generation of bachelors even managed to pull, armed with little more than a packet of beef risotto and a bottle of Mateus Rosc.

But you certainly couldn't have called any of the varieties 'ready meals' – they were distinctly unready, taking twenty-

five minutes to cook. In the case of the still-chewy carrots, peas and peppers that you ended up with, twenty-four hours of cooking time might have produced a better result. No wonder, after all that slaving, we deserted the dinner table and lapped up our re-hydrated feast slumped in front of Mike Yarwood or *George and Mildred*. The TV dinner was born.

What do you mean, chopsticks?

Vesta meals might have come in small packets, but they left a mountain of washing up. In the case of the Chow Mein with Crispy Noodles: two frying pans, a saucepan, a plate, utensils and a knife and fork. (No, we didn't know how to use chopsticks.) We had absolutely no idea that in less than half an hour you could easily stir-fry some delicious fresh meat and vegetables.

Vesta was eventually rumbled by consumers as they became more knowledgeable and adventurous. The list of dried ingredients does now read a little like a chemical experiment – including two different flavour enhancers. By the 1980s, we could no longer wait half an hour for a packet meal. Vesta's makers were already onto 'instant noodle' type products, which rehydrated in minutes. Yet the fact remains that Vesta blazed a trail, paving the way for today's global industry dedicated to complete prepared meals – whether in packets, tins, chilled or frozen. In other words, Vesta has to take the blame for the Death of Proper Cooking.

GALE'S HONEY

Marmalade might be the traditional accompaniment to our morning toast, but honey wears the crown when it comes to nostalgic appeal. Despite the fact that it's been eaten the world over for thousands of years it somehow feels so English. It's probably all to do with A.A. Milne and Rupert Brooke (although, to modern ears, ten to three does sound rather early to be having your tea, let alone honey) or maybe it's about childhood memories of drinking hot lemon and honey when we were poorly. Whatever the reason, and despite the fact that 'teatime' has all but disappeared for anyone over the age of eight, we still manage to eat 25,000 tonnes of honey every year between us.

The bee's knees

Today, the array on offer at your average supermarket can make choosing a pot a bewildering business. Gone is the time when all we had to do was opt for 'clear' or 'set'. Now there's every flavour from Acacia to Wild Thyme, some commercially farmed, others produced by 'artisans'; the merits of organic versus non-organic

have to be considered, not to mention the vexed question of whether or not we want honeycomb in it. All that before we even think about the carbon footprint: should we really be buying honey which has travelled all the way from Tasmania or China? And is Romania nearer to Kent than Poland?

Fortunate enough to have a grandfather who kept bees, Philippa never tasted commercially produced honey until she was a teenager, and barely recognized it as such when she did. Pale, slimy and tasteless, it bore little resemblance to the dense, strongly scented nectar she was used to. Granted, you didn't bend the spoon digging it out of the jar and no, it never crystallized so hard that you had to run the lid under a hot tap to get it off, but she still didn't like it. For most people in the 1970s,

Survivability	*8/10*
Trolley Embarrassment Factor	*3/10*
Versatility	*HIGH*

however, honey came from a shop — and the chances are it was Gale's.

The end is nigh

Gale's hive-shaped jars of honey first appeared in 1919 and then, as now, contained a blend of honeys imported from various countries. The company sells about four-and-a-half million jars a year but the unpredictable British climate has long meant that we eat far more honey than we can produce for ourselves. Now, our average yield is down to about 4,000 tonnes in a normal year — less than a fifth of what we buy. A toxic cocktail of wet summers, the parasitic Varroa mite and the disastrous phenomenon known as 'colony collapse disorder' has killed off about two billion British bees in the past year alone. It's the same sad story in many other parts of the world and the price of honey is rising.

Jam yesterday

Couldn't we have something different for a change? they said. And then she thought back to her childhood. Long, lazy summer afternoons. Tea outside with a crusty farmhouse loaf, fresh yellow butter . . . and honey.

Honey, rich and golden and beautiful. Just like Gale's honey today. Honey harvested from the finest hives in the world. Nothing added, nothing taken away. One of the greatest natural sources of energy. Is there a jar of sunshine in *your* house?

Honey-one of the greatest foods of all time

For people old enough to have lived through the Second World War, all this has a familiar ring. Unlike sugar, honey was never rationed, but it was hard to find and expensive. A honey substitute called Sunny Spread did make an appearance but no one seems to remember it fondly.

The end of British honey might seem an inconsequential inconvenience compared to recent global shortages of essential foods, but it's worth remembering that bees play a part in about a third of all the food we eat and Einstein reckoned that man would only have four years of life left if they disappeared entirely. So let's hope the government breaks out the piggy bank the next time angry beekeepers march on Downing Street demanding cash for apian research because we don't know about you, but we've got plans for 2014.

EAT ME DATES

Nowadays it's hard to know when the festive season actually begins: August? September? It's anybody's guess. But in the days before retailers realized they could sell us what used to be seasonal products all year round, we knew. Back then Christmas was coming when, much like the first crocuses of spring, boxes of Eat Me Dates would suddenly appear, poking out between the bananas and the pineapples in the local greengrocer's. Back then, like the red string bags of impenetrable nuts, Eat Me Dates were an essential Christmas treat.

Take me to the Kasbah

Sad to say, however, Eat Me Dates were always a bit of a disappointment. The glossy and succulent fruit pictured on the lid, promised an exotic, even erotic, eating experience which the contents utterly failed to deliver. Fiendishly difficult to extract from the box, even with the aid of the plastic spear provided, each glutinous mouthful somehow involved too little date and too much stone. Nevertheless, in the early 1970s Eat Me Dates had an air of mystery about them. Like Fry's Turkish Delight, they conjured up visions of sexily veiled houris with kohl-rimmed eyes. In truth, the real mystery lay in who actually ate them. When exactly is a good moment to consume a sticky date soaked in glucose syrup? Before the turkey, with a festive gin and tonic? Hardly. Afterwards, with a glass of port? Possibly, but wouldn't you rather have an After Eight? Which is why the box of Eat Me's always lingered hopefully on the sideboard long after the January sales had been and gone.

Today, the dates do seem a little plumper, the pack has been modernized and they have dispensed with the plastic spear, but the skin still has a tendency to slough off the date and wallpaper itself to your teeth. Not nice. All this is a bit of a

Survivability	*2/10*
Trolley Embarrassment Factor	*7/10*
Versatility	*LOW*

pity because dates can be delicious. As far back as 5000 BC, the nomads of North Africa and the Middle East did a roaring trade in them, and earthenware jars of dates have even been found in the tombs of Pharaohs. Rich in fibre, vitamins and minerals, they're said to have kept the desert-dwelling Bedouin going for months on end, with nothing more than camel's milk to wash them down. Each to their own.

What's in a name?

It's difficult to see a long-term market for a product as, well,

dated, as Eat Me Dates. That whiff of the kazbah is nothing new to well-travelled twenty-first-century consumers, and that tooth-aching sweetness is just too cloying for modern palates. As for the name … we can only assume that when Eat Me Dates were new the brand name didn't have the less-than-family-friendly connotations it conjures up today. Nowadays the inquiry 'Eat Me?' (however politely put) is unlikely to involve a sticky date – well, not that kind of sticky date. Enough said.

All round the Clock

there's always time for NESCAFÉ

Now for a good cup of coffee with roaster-fresh fragrance, full-bodied flavour! Just the coffee you like. The special Nestlé process seals in aroma and flavour until the touch of hot water releases it— lively, fresh, appetising. Whether you add milk and sugar to taste or serve it black, you'll agree it's the coffee for you.

Nescafé is a soluble coffee product composed of coffee solids, combined and powdered with dextrins, maltose and dextrose added to protect the flavour.

ANOTHER OF NESTLÉ'S GOOD THINGS

NESCAFÉ

It was eighty years ago when Brazilian coffee producers asked Nestlé's Swiss boffins if they could help reduce the country's vast surplus by creating a product made from a concentrated solution of real coffee with the water removed. It took a research team eight years to do it. But eventually, a factory in Hayes, Middlesex was turning out Nescafé, and during the Second World War it became a staple drink for the US military.

The power of advertising

Nestlé soon had competition, notably from Maxwell House, who first came up with freeze-dried coffee, using a different drying process that produced a superior flavour. What really seems to have boosted demand for instant was that the ad breaks on the new commercial television channel just weren't long enough for people to go out to the kitchen and make a proper pot of tea.

Eventually, we began to travel and started experiencing European café culture for ourselves. Back home, corner cafés spooning powdered instant out of a catering tin were slow to adapt and were rapidly replaced by Identikit branches of Starbucks, Costa, and the rest.

Nescafé's most celebrated advertising pitch was its long-running TV campaign for Gold Blend, in which that smug-looking pair Sharon Maughan and Anthony Head, spent a decade popping into each other's apartments to borrow coffee. It was all farcical misunderstandings and sexual tension, with the two never quite getting it on until 1993, when more than 30 million people tuned in to see Anthony's character finally express his undying love. These days, heart throb actor George Clooney is a poster boy for the latest Nespresso coffee pod machines, but the British alone still drink 15,000 cups of Nescafé every single minute. One way or another, Nestlé seems to have it covered.

Survivability	9/10
Trolley Embarrassment Factor	5/10
Versatility	MEDIUM

BIRDS EYE FISH FINGERS

There must be people out there who don't like fish fingers, but have you ever met one? Quite what it is that makes this teatime food so acceptable is an interesting question, because there's not much to it, just white fish fried in breadcrumbs. But perhaps it's that very simplicity that is the secret of fish fingers' success – you know what you're going to get when you set to work on a plateful and that's very reassuring. A dash of ketchup or tartare sauce; a squeeze of lemon; some decent chips or a plate of bread and butter: sorted.

In 2005, on the fiftieth anniversary of their launch, it emerged that an astonishing 15 billion fish fingers had been sold, and by then we were getting through more than a million a day. Captain Birdseye actor John Hewer may have spent

Survivability	*9/10*
Trolley Embarrassment Factor	*3/10*
Versatility	*LOW*

thirty years of his life persuading kids to eat them, but the truth is that two-thirds of all fish fingers are scoffed by grown-ups (not to mention all the ones our kids leave on their plates which we feel morally obliged to polish off as well ...).

Avast me hearties ...
But salty old seadog Captain Birdseye (or Captain Igloo as he's known to our continental cousins), did teach the marketeers a thing or two when they pensioned him off in 1997. Replacement actor Thomas Pescod might have been younger and tastier but he didn't cut any ice with children, and four years later Birds Eye made him walk the plank, hiring a Hewer lookalike to do the job instead.

We have the delightfully named Clarence Birdseye to thank for fish fingers. An American scientist, he cottoned on to just how fast fish can freeze while working as a biologist in Canada. By the late 1920s he'd patented both a quick-freezing process and the product, and 'fish sticks' were soon being sold in the US by a company called Gortons, which still sells them to this day. Here in Britain, H. A. J. Scott of Great Yarmouth started making cod fish fingers in 1955 after singularly failing to convince housewives in Southampton and South Wales that a version made with herring was delicious. During the market-testing

No stowaways aboard.

Birds Eye Cod Fillet Fish Fingers have only 100% natural ingredients. No artificial colours or flavourings.

exercise, shoppers overwhelmingly gave the thumbs up to a cod version, which had only been included as a control. H. A. J. Scott took the hint, 'Herring Savouries' were dumped, and the women working in the factory voted for 'Fish Fingers' as the new product name. History doesn't relate what they did with the herrings.

Just like mum used to make?

Some people think that fish fingers are thinner than they used to be, so we cooked some up to find out. At first glance we tended to agree, but we can't be sure about this, not having a twenty-year-old packet to compare them with. We also thought the breadcrumbs looked chunkier than they used to be, and darker, but this could have been because Nigel burnt them. One thing you can be pretty confident about is that your fish fingers won't contain any bones. Apparently, the giant blocks of frozen fish used to make them are x-rayed before they're sliced up.

Every bite's **double delicious**...
because there's **fresh chunky fish inside,**
crispy-golden breadcrumbs outside.
Only Birds Eye make a Fish Finger so good.

BIRDS EYE

QUICK-FROZEN FISH FINGERS

BIRDS EYE FISH FINGERS – the true taste of good food

In recent years, diminishing cod stocks in the North Sea have forced producers to turn to other white fish varieties. They're making a virtue out of necessity by highlighting the fact that Omega 3 (a dietary must-have for children) occurs at higher levels in Alaskan pollock than in cod. All very laudable, but it does make buying fish fingers something of an ethical minefield, because now you and your kids have to decide which fish stocks you want to save, and which you're happy to endanger. No pressure then.

HEINZ SANDWICH SPREAD

Survivability	2/10
Trolley Embarrassment Factor	9/10
Versatility	LOW

You may be surprised to hear that Heinz Sandwich Spread hasn't died and gone to product heaven along with Funny Feet ice creams or Chef Square Shaped Soup. Those green-labelled jars of chopped celery, carrot, gherkin and red pepper suspended in a mayonnaisey sauce are hanging on in there, along with their elderly cousins Toast Toppers and Salad Cream.

Mums thought using Sandwich Spread was an easy way to stuff healthy veg into their kids. Impressively, Heinz Sandwich Spread has a forty-two per cent vegetable content. Less impressively, the standard variety is heavy on fat and the label suggests it contains negligible fibre, which only makes you wonder how they manage to remove it all from the forty-two per cent of vegetables.

Not for fashionistas

Sadly, Sandwich Spread is no longer fashionable – it's become the sandwich filling equivalent of loon pants. But its pleasantly crunchy in a small way – in fact, if you added mustard powder to Sandwich Spread, it would turn out rather like piccalilli run through a blender. The trouble was once we had gone abroad and tasted freshly made bruschettas, a gloop of what amounts to bumpy mayo on white bread was hardly going to get the party started.

As kids in the 1970s we did have a descriptive if entirely undeserved nickname for Sandwich Spread. We won't spell it out, but here's a clue: if the product reminds you of the pavement in front of your local kebab shop on a Sunday morning, it really is time you stopped going clubbing.

Thirty years ago, anything made a change from the endless sandwich fillings of processed cheese, corned beef or luncheon meat. Now, most of us can barely be bothered to butter bread, let alone make our own sandwiches every morning. We're told about seven million prepared sandwiches are eaten daily. In these retro times, surely there must be room for Sandwich Spread in at least a few of them?

LEA & PERRINS WORCESTERSHIRE SAUCE

Millions of British households have a bottle of tangy Lea & Perrins Worcestershire Sauce quietly maturing in the larder. Sporting its old-fashioned, long-necked bottle, that traditional orange label and typeface, not to mention the Royal Appointment crest, it really could have been sitting on a shelf minding its own business since Victorian times.

In a UK TV Food survey, Lea & Perrins Worcestershire Sauce was voted Britain's finest contribution to world cuisine, coming in ahead of Cheddar cheese, Yorkshire pudding and clotted cream. Technically, it's not so much a sauce as a fermented condiment – nothing touches its complex, spicy sweet-saltiness to wake up a Bloody Mary, enliven a stew, or soup-up a soup. Some people couldn't contemplate eating cheese-on-toast without it.

For more than a century, the red-brick factory in Midland Road has infused the neighbourhood with the aroma of more exotic climes than downtown Worcester – anchovies from the Mediterranean, tamarind from India, chilli peppers from Africa. It's the whole world captured in a bottle and left to ferment for eighteen months in wooden casks. A valiant band of just thirty-five workers turn out some 28 million bottles a year. Owners Heinz say it's an efficient production site and they've no plans to shift it abroad (as they did with HP Sauce).

An exotic history

The history long put out by Lea & Perrins is a belter. Home from his travels in India, Lord Marcus Sandys, a Worcestershire nobleman (most accounts say he was a former Governor of Bengal) commissioned chemists John Lea and William Perrins to try to duplicate a favourite recipe that he had brought back with him. Unfortunately, when brewed, the concoction smelled and tasted horrible and was consigned to the cellar to gather dust.

Survivability	*10/10*
Trolley Embarrassment Factor	*0/10*
Versatility	*HIGH*

Fortunately, the chemists tasted it years later – to discover that the aging process had produced a delicious, piquant sauce. So, in 1837, Mr Lea and Mr Perrins started bottling it, and within a few years it was known and coveted in kitchens throughout Europe.

This history has been swallowed whole by some distinguished food writers but, sadly, the truth may not be as spicy. There's no record of a Lord Sandys ever having governed Bengal, or even having been in India. Nonetheless, Lea & Perrins are sticking with the story, which they say has grown up as part of the business. The fact is there's no strong evidence either way, so maybe we shouldn't blame them for keeping it alive.

Known the world over

Goodness knows what all those export customers do with the stuff. The Spanish use it in vinaigrettes, they put it on tortillas in El Salvador, and it's become a staple ingredient in Asian cuisine. Another vast market is America, where the bottles now display the less-than-classy slogan 'The Burger Booster' – which gives some clue as to what American cooks like to do with Worcestershire Sauce. Just don't ask them to pronounce it.

Once you've tried it, you'll never cook without it

Lea and Perrins Worcester Sauce adds dash to your cooking

You're used to shaking Lea and Perrins Worcester Sauce onto savoury food, so you'll know it's the tastiest sauce in the world – sharp-sweet and deliciously piquant. But when you use it in slow cooking you can stir in a whole tablespoonful, two – or even more. Simmering mellows the tang of Lea and Perrins Worcester Sauce until it's a natural part of the dish. A casserole or a pie becomes richer, more interesting; gravy or soups gain an indefinably delicious flavour. Welsh rarebit glows with taste!

Lea & Perrins bottles turn up everywhere – encrusted with barnacles on shipwrecks, buried in the rubble of an 1886 volcanic eruption in New Zealand, and even discovered in the hidden Tibetan city of Lhasa. It's also a popular – if scientifically unproven – hangover cure. P.G. Wodehouse's fictional butler, Jeeves, famously prescribes an over-refreshed Bertie Wooster with a mixture of Worcestershire Sauce, raw egg and pepper. As he put it himself: 'Gentlemen have told me they find it extremely invigorating after a late evening'. You'll have to try that one for yourself.

MUSHY PEAS

The young Peter (now Lord) Mandelson is in his parliamentary constituency in the north of England, trying to reinforce his working class credentials. He goes into a fish and chip shop, where he spies a dish of mushy peas on the back counter. 'Cod and chips, please … Oh, and I'll have some of that guacamole over there …'

It's an old joke now, yet neatly illustrates what used to be a distinct north-south divide in the matter of pea consumption. While us Southerners had discovered frozen peas and become acquainted with avocados, our northern cousins were still partnering their fish or pie and chips with good old mushy peas. Yet more recently, we soft Southerners have seen the light. Mushy peas have been promoted to the gastronomic high ground to become a totemic British vegetable.

Comfort food

Mushy peas – or the unsquashed, skin-shedding marrowfat version if you must – are the yummiest and most comforting vegetable to eat at any time of year. And certainly the most luminous, since most processed peas owe their improbable green hue to two notorious artificial colours, E102 and E133, which have been long been living on borrowed time. Some own-label brands are now produced without them, but it has to be said that while processed peas are more wholesome au naturel, the undyed, grey-looking veg in the cans does take some getting used to. And yes, we do know that, technically, the pea is a fruit – it's the seed pod of a legume. But it's treated as a vegetable in cooking, so let's give that one a rest.

Mushy peas are produced by drying peas after harvesting and shipping them to a processing plant, where they are soaked overnight in water and a little bicarbonate of soda is added to soften them and inhibit fermentation. This, apparently, makes them less likely to give us flatulence. The peas are then simmered with sugar and salt, and sometimes mint may be added for flavouring, before the product is put into cans.

Napoleon's idea

Strangely, the French prefer non-processed 'garden' peas in tins to either mushy or even frozen peas. For a nation of foodies, this is inexplicable. Maybe France's loyalty to tinned peas is in homage to the man who made them possible – Napoleon Bonaparte. He knew that successful armies marched on their stomachs, and offered 12,000 Francs to anyone who could successfully preserve food in containers. It was a Parisian confectioner, Nicolas Appert, who won the prize in 1795, having perfected a laborious five-hour process in which meat or vegetables were heated to boiling point and sealed in glass jars. French naval officials reported that Appert's beans and green peas had 'all the freshness and the agreeable flavour of freshly picked vegetables'. Yeah, right.

Nearer home, a Bermondsey company, Donkin and Hall, pioneered using tin-plate cans – winning massive orders from the Admiralty. At the time, peas were well suited to canning because all the food had to be pushed through a small hole in the top of the can, which was sealed with a soldered disc. By the 1860s, processes had improved and canned food was on offer to the masses, although it was our more commercially minded cousins in America who came up with the idea of coloured pictorial labels showing what was inside.

As far as we know, only once have tinned peas presented our nation with a threat. In 1940, a three-man team of German agents was caught with cans of peas containing nitrocellulose, which they planned to use to blow up Buckingham Palace.

Today, Premier Foods dominate the tinned pea universe, with their Batchelors' brand. Many of us are content with a supermarket version, and just keep a tin or two 'for emergencies'. The bulk of the peas we eat may come frozen these days, but it is good to know that the mushy variety retain some nutrients after processing. We're told you could actually survive on them for some time without your hair or teeth falling out, although such a diet would surely leave you feeling more than a little green.

Survivability	8/10
Trolley Embarrassment Factor	8/10
Versatility	LOW

OXO

A friend of ours admits she was devastated to discover that the Oxo Family she'd watched on TV for years were not a real family. It was in 1999 that actress Lynda Bellingham and her fake 'husband' finally moved house, after warming the nation's cockles for fifteen years with their kitchen table banter. The original Oxo mum was the sweet natured if sanitized Katie, who slaved over a hot stove for sixteen years.

Fluid beef

Oxo originally had the less catchy name of Liebig's Meat Extract – described as 'fluid beef', a term that would give today's EU food chiefs apoplexy. Justus von Liebig had written of the dangers of boiling meat and destroying its goodness. He developed a concentrated extract, though it was his chief chemist who turned Oxo

into dissolvable cubes that were packed in tins and sold for one penny. As to where the name came from, one not entirely plausible story is that a docker chalked O-X-O on a crate to identify it, though it's just as likely 'Ox' was simply a reference to the animal.

Poor people who couldn't afford beef loved the notion of an extract containing all the goodness of meat. But frankly a cube contains more wheat flour, salt, yeast extract, cornflour and flavour enhancers than anything beefy.

When chicken meets new Golden Oxo something sumptuous happens

Chicken always was good. But now it's downright sumptuous. Because now you can buy Golden Oxo to go with it.

New Golden Oxo is a second kind of Oxo cube. One that's specially made to bring out the delicate flavour of the "light" meats—like chicken, pork and veal. And to keep their light colour, too.

Next time you buy a chicken, give it Golden Oxo gravy. Or try the recipe given on the left.

Get your Golden Oxo today!

Golden Chicken with Almonds

Coat 4 chicken pieces with seasoned flour. Fry in oil till brown all over. Add Golden Oxo stock (1 Golden Oxo cube dissolved—not crumbled—in ½ pt. hot water). Cover, and cook gently till tender —about 1 hour. Add ¼ pt. double cream, 1 oz. chopped salted almonds and 2 teasps. horseradish sauce, and heat to boiling. Delectable! (4 servings.)

WITH BOTH KINDS OF OXO OXO OXO YOUR LARDER'S COMPLETE

In 1920, Liebig acquired the site of an old power station on the south bank of the river Thames and built the famous Oxo tower. Permission to put up illuminated signs was refused, so instead the windows and bricks at the top were designed so they just happened to be in the shapes of a circle, a cross and a circle – neatly spelling out the word O-X-O.

In 2002, the nation's bean-counters unsportingly threw stock cubes out of the official basket of frequently purchased goods used to calculate High Street inflation. Maybe it's time to bring the old Oxo family out of retirement.

Survivability	*4/10*
Trolley Embarrassment Factor	*6/10*
Versatility	*HIGH*

CARNATION EVAPORATED MILK

Older people insist to this day on keeping a tin or two of evap in the larder. The shame attached to running out of milk is deeply ingrained into the British. We also like to be fully prepared for any unspecified civil emergencies that might require the immediate preparation of an evaporated milk mousse whipped up with a table jelly. Because half the water had been removed, evaporated milk was really rich at a time when fresh cream was for special occasions only. The high heat process also lent evap that pleasantly caramelized flavour. We never gave a thought to the doubled calorie and fat content.

Choppy beginnings

Pioneers had been trying to heat milk to preserve it since the 1820s, but it always had a scorched taste. In 1852, Gail Borden, a young Texan dairy farmer, politician and inventor, was on a ship heading home from visiting the Great Exhibition at Crystal Palace. It is said that the sea was so rough that the cows on board were seasick and couldn't be milked. Borden

This famous Milk is now partially released for domestic use. More ample supplies will become available as conditions improve.

saw his potential market. When he got home, he managed to evaporate milk slowly in a vacuum, using a copper kettle – although the process did involve adding sugar to aid preservation.

The Carnation company was founded at the turn of the century by wholesale grocer Elbridge Amos Stuart. He'd moved to Washington State, taking over a failing business in the new town of Kent. Teaming up with a clever industry veteran named John Baptist Meyenber, he ditched the sugar and improved the sterilization and canning processes.

He was also fanatical about his dairy herd, advertising from 1907 that his Carnation milk came from 'contented cows'. That phrase on the label always troubled us. How could they be sure the cows were content to give away all their milk? More

worryingly, did it also mean all cows without the Carnation contract were fed up?

Tinned milk remains essential wherever fresh is hard to find. It's also popular with commercial caterers. One let slip to us that evap is used in first-class airline meals because it's more stable than cream when reheated at 38,000 feet. Now there's one use even the visionary Gail Borden couldn't have dreamt of on his choppy, milk-free sea voyage across the Atlantic.

Survivability	*6/10*
Trolley Embarrassment Factor	*6/10*
Versatility	*HIGH*

CONDENSED SOUP

If you go down the tinned soup aisle today, you're sure of a big surprise. One of the most famous canned products in the world no longer sports its familiar red-and-white Campbell's label with the little gold medal. Campbell's in America obviously thinks the glory days are over for tinned soup – it's gone and sold the recipes to Premier Foods. So that's why the tins now say 'Batchelors' – the same name that adorns Super Noodles and, er, Cup-a-Soup. Oh dear.

Heavy water

Condensed soup was invented at the turn of the century, when a gifted chemist, John Torrance, discovered how to drive out half of the heaviest ingredient – water. The trick was to use a strong stock that held its flavour when you added an equal amount of water. Torrance's uncle happened to be a partner at Campbell's, a preserved foods company in New Jersey, USA, and his innovation cut the costs of soup packaging and shipping by two-thirds.

Over the years Campbell's have come up with plenty of suggestions for lobbing the soup undiluted into recipes. But it's hard to imagine many people making Tomato Soup Cake more than once.

Pop art

Some people are clearly missing Campbell's already because they've been bidding good money for the old-label British tins on eBay. But it's not clear whether they just eat their auction purchase for lunch, or arrange the cans on a shelf to create their very own

Just what a good meal should contain!

The iron of the green vegetables
The valuable mineral salts
The nourishment of cereals
The invigoration of beef broth
An invitation to your appetite
A satisfaction to your hunger

21 kinds   12 cents a can

Campbell's SOUPS

LOOK FOR THE RED AND WHITE LABEL

Warhol-style art installation. (Apparently, Andy's mum gave him tomato soup almost every day for twenty years. No wonder he resorted to painting pictures of the cans between meals.)

So next time you pass an old grocery store, don't forget to see if you can make your fortune by snapping up a few old Campbell's soup cans languishing on the back of a shelf. Who knows, you might also spot some priceless and long lost Marathon Bars or Opal Fruits while you're there.

Survivability	*4/10*
Trolley Embarrassment Factor	*6/10*
Versatility	*MEDIUM*

HORLICKS

What a sleep-deprived nation we have become: a third of us manage less than six hours' kip a night. No wonder we love our HMDs – that's advertising-speak for Hot Milky Drinks. Just as well the inventors of Horlicks changed the name from their first effort, which they called Diastoid, making it sound like a hideous illness or a treatment for haemorrhoids.

Smell that steam

We used to love those industrial-sized Horlicks mixers behind seaside café counters – dispensing a sea of thick white foam, complete with a few toffee-like globs that stuck to the roof of your mouth. Those scalding, hard-to-hold, branded mugs with no hole in the handle for little fingers were also part of the authentic experience. It was all warm, sweet, malty and comforting as you cleared the condensation off the window to look out at the driving Bank Holiday rain. Never mind that a mug of the original formulation packs around the same number of calories as a Cadbury's Creme Egg.

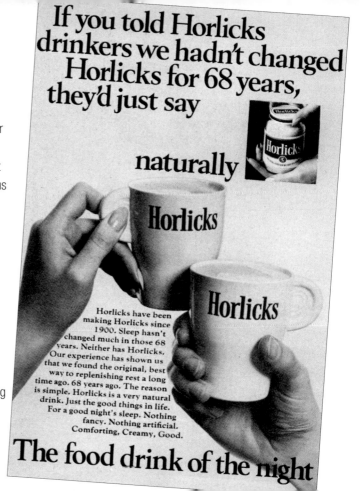

If you told Horlicks drinkers we hadn't changed Horlicks for 68 years, they'd just say

naturally

Horlicks have been making Horlicks since 1900. Sleep hasn't changed much in those 68 years. Neither has Horlicks. Our experience has shown us that we found the original, best way to replenishing rest a long time ago, 68 years ago. The reason is simple. Horlicks is a very natural drink. Just the good things in life. For a good night's sleep. Nothing fancy. Nothing artificial. Comforting, Creamy, Good.

The food drink of the night

Horlicks was dreamed up by two brothers from the Forest of Dean in Gloucestershire. William Horlick emigrated to the United States in 1869 and his pharmacist brother James joined him four years later. The plan was to produce a patented malt drink for infants. It was so successful the pair soon had their own factory in Wisconsin, where they perfected the art of mixing malted barley and wheat with fresh milk and water and evaporating the mixture into the famous off-white powder. By 1908, James had returned to England, bought land from Eton College and built a factory in Stoke Poges Lane, Slough – now regarded as the town's most beautiful landmark. Well, it certainly is if you've ever seen Slough Bus Station.

There's even a mountain named after it

Since it was lightweight, high in calories and didn't go off, Horlicks was soon being taken on expeditions – lending its name to the Horlicks Mountains in the Antarctic. James was made a baronet and died in July 1921. In 1945 the US and UK businesses were reunited, and early in 1969 Horlicks was sold for £20 million to what's become the multinational pharmaceutical giant GlaxoSmithKline (GSK). It says something about the cost of developing blockbuster medicines if GSK still think they can do just as well with Horlicks.

We have the former British Foreign Secretary Jack Straw to thank for memorably describing an official document on Iraqi weapons of mass destruction as 'a complete Horlicks'. Mind you, it's not just government dossiers being sexed up. Now they're definitely trying to sex up Horlicks itself, with a big push to ensure it is served to post-partying WAGS in fashionable hotels and clubs. For us, though, it's more about Grandma – resplendent in her pink winceyette dressing gown and curlers, enjoying a bedtime cup with Reginald Bosanquet on *News At Ten*. So you won't catch us ordering Horlicks in a hip bar after a long night partying in the mosh-pit.

Survivability	*4/10*
Trolley Embarrassment Factor	*10/10*
Versatility	*LOW*

MR BRAIN'S FAGGOTS

Faggots are the jokers in the freezer cabinet and you hardly ever see them prominently displayed. The name alone is enough to put some people off their dinner. Yet the day that Mr Brain's Pork Faggots finally disappear, you can be sure that the sun will have finally set on the British Empire.

Faggots are a kind of English haggis – originally made from minced liver and heart combined with onions, seasoning and breadcrumbs soaked in milk. As with haggis, they magically transform animal parts that would otherwise go to waste into an edible dish. As the old saying goes: you can eat all of the pig except the squeal. Faggots were even excluded from the wartime meat ration.

Most popular in the West Midlands, Wales, parts of the West Country and the North, faggots were often bought from butchers – sometimes going under the alternative name of savoury ducks. Each was wrapped in its own little jacket made from caul, which was taken from pig's innards. Often they were cooked in a crock and served deliciously warm and comforting with peas, yellow split peas or mashed potato.

Mind your language

Faggot is the Latin word for 'bundle'. In the United States, faggot is a slang word for something entirely different. Skilfully, the current owners of Mr Brain's, the Kerry Group, have managed to steer the product through this potential minefield with some playful advertising. In doing so, they have significantly raised sales to the present 14 million packs a year. However, Kerry has never gone as far as the Somerfield supermarket chain, which daringly commissioned a radio ad featuring a husband challenging his partner's repetitive menus with the words: 'I've nothing against faggots, I just don't fancy

Survivability	**5/10**
Trolley Embarrassment Factor	**3/10**
Versatility	**LOW**

them.' Never noted for its rollicking sense of humour, OFCOM ruled that the ad breached taste and decency rules, and promptly banned it.

The original Mr Brain was Herbert Hill Brain, the son of a grocer who had established his own wholesale provisions business in Bristol. By the 1930s, Brain's was using a site in Upper York Street for curing its own bacon and hams. It was one of the workers who came up with the idea of making faggots, and soon they became Brain's best-known product. The business later passed through several hands, one of which unsportingly sold the Bristol site before going bust. So Kerry had to move production to Enniskillen in Northern Ireland, but took some old West Country hands with them to ensure authenticity.

Trendsetting

Surprisingly, faggots have yet to become trendy. That's in spite of the efforts of offal-loving chefs like Fergus Henderson, who runs the fashionable St John Restaurant in London. Maybe they will soon, now food shoppers are actively looking for sources of inexpensive protein. Supermarkets are seeing rising demand for

liver, kidneys and the like, and faggot-based ready meals have been sighted at Waitrose.

As to what Mr Brain's taste like, well they are surprisingly light compared to home-made faggots, the flavour somewhat reminiscent of stuffing. But it does help if – like us – you actively like liver. If you're the sort of wimp who doesn't, you might find yourself pushing your plate away, mildly concerned about that slight twang at the back of your palate. Don't say we didn't warn you.

SHIPPAM'S FISH PASTE

If you're under the age of forty, the chances are you've never tasted fish paste, let alone bought it. In fact, if you're a keen angler you may be labouring under the misapprehension that it's something you use as bait, but that's fishing paste. In pre-fridge days, when eating fish more than a couple of days old was like a cheap version of Russian roulette (in that you might die but you didn't have to go to the expense of buying a gun), the little glass jars were a national institution. Unless you lived by the sea, it was probably the nearest you ever got to a crab.

Pastes, made from a percentage of ground fish mixed with cereal or other fillers, are our inheritance from the Victorian afternoon tea table. Every taste is catered for, from homely Bloater and Pilchard Pastes to upmarket Anchovy or even Potted Salmon and Crab. Firm favourites all, despite their off-putting hues, variations of the colour Jeremy Clarkson once memorably described as 'hearing aid beige'. Before television was invented, families whiled away happy hours trying vainly to tell one flavour from another.

A potted history

Founded in the late 1700s, Shippam's has seen off a host of local and national competitors and the name remains synonymous with 'fish paste'. Established in Chichester by one Charles Shippam, the business began as a humble grocery and expanded over the next century into a butchers shop and a potted meat factory. Exactly when Shippam's began using fish isn't clear, but with the English Channel on the doorstep it would have been plain silly not to, and Shippam's pastes are made in Chichester to this day.

In 1905, the famous ribbed glass jars and sealed metal lids came in and the company began sterilizing the products to make them last longer. Protected as we are now by a fortress of food safety regulations, it's hard to imagine how hazardous food could be before the science of preserving it was properly understood. In the 1800s, fish products were responsible for some notorious health disasters. Ever keen to find plausible and unobtrusive ways to finish people off, murder mystery writers regularly poisoned their hapless victims with noxious substances cunningly concealed in fish-paste sandwiches. Agatha Christie was particularly prone to the habit, employing fish paste on several occasions as a possible murder weapon – and even as a red herring (if you'll pardon the pun).

Down, Bimbo!

As food technology improved, the health risks diminished and public confidence grew. Shippam's was among the first companies to advertise on TV – daringly showing paste sandwiches being served at a tea party, in a lunch box and to guests, with the voiceover: 'It's hard to see how you could do without Shippam's pastes'. But in spite of Shippam's efforts, fish paste started

At the sign of the Wish-bone

A mound of chicken wish-bones—hundreds of thousands of them—is a sight you might well see if you were to visit the Shippam factory at Chichester. Every week thousands of fine plump chickens are delivered to the factory. They are typical of the fresh top-grade ingredients that go into Shippam's meat and fish pastes and all their other fine foods…maintaining a tradition of quality that has been handed down from father to son for more than 200 years.

Shippam's

BY APPOINTMENT TO H.H. THE QUEEN, SUPPLIERS OF MEAT AND FISH PASTES. C. SHIPPAM LTD.

AT CHICHESTER SINCE 1750

to fall out of favour with the more affluent, though it remained popular until the late 1960s for feeding a crowd. Nigel well remembers the day from his childhood when the family cat, Bimbo, got into the nearby church hall, discovered a plate of fish-paste rolls prepared for a party and managed to lick the fishy filling off at least half a dozen before the crime was discovered. A friend also recalls visits to a pair of great-aunts where tea invariably featured little fish-paste sandwiches; apparently the house always smelt slightly odd and she never discovered if the sandwiches or the aunts were to blame.

Fifty years on, with a fridge in every home and telly nutritionists and chefs constantly hammering home the advantages of freshly prepared food, fish paste has become synonymous with all that is vilified about the post-war British diet. Perceived as bland, old-fashioned food that you'd only serve to your granny if you didn't want her to come to tea again any time soon, it's hard to see how manufacturers can win over younger consumers. Undeterred, the colossal Mitsubishi Corporation has high hopes for Shippam's, which it now controls as part of its Princes Group. The last member of the Shippam family retired in 1998, but the Japanese people are, of course, no strangers to fish paste. Their version, surimi – which involves puréed white fish masquerading as shellfish – is enjoyed all over the world, not least here in the UK where you may know it better as … 'crabsticks'. Then again, when did you last eat one of those?

Survivability	1/10
Trolley Embarrassment Factor	10/10
Versatility	LOW

Who When & Where

by ROBERT SERRE

My enthusiasm for cooking extends far beyond my job as Head Chef in a London club and I was delighted when Shippam's asked me to help them in the development of their Supreme Range. Now that all four of these are on sale, it seems a good idea to pass on to you the recipes we use in our own home.

Just to show how these recipes can help you solve some family eating problems, I'll tell you how I came to make them, who ate them and when. We're a perfectly ordinary family, two daughters, one married and the other at University, and one son who is still at home. My wife, Joyce, does most of the cooking but I quite often help out because I enjoy it.

But first of all, I'd like to tell you something about the Supreme Range itself. All four cans are quite distinctive in their own ways, so that any recipe I give you is really four recipes, because if you use a different can from the one I suggest you'll get another exciting dish. For instance Chicken Supreme, Chicken Continental and Chicken American all have fine plump chunks of chicken in them, but whereas Chicken Supreme has a delicate, creamy white sauce, Chicken Continental is more piquant in the French manner – it reminds you of holidays abroad! American

↑ Me and my family

has a creamy sauce blended with tomato and a dash of lemon – quite different again. Turkey Supreme, in addition to generous chunks of turkey meat, has a sauce into which herbs have been blended – among lots of other things – to bring out the true flavour of turkey.

Before you start making any of these into recipes, why not try them on their own first? They're all delicious as they are, hot or cold. Next time you want to eat in a hurry try one of them piping hot, on toast – or for a fuller meal, with vegetables. They're good for picnics too – easy to carry and delicious with salad. Or if you don't want to mess about with plates, Supreme sandwiches take some beating. So you see, the Supreme range is very versatile, even before you start the real fun of cooking.

Shippam's CHICKEN SUPREME Shippam's CHICKEN AMERICAN Shippam's TURKEY SUPREME Shippam's CHICKEN CONTINENTAL

ALL IN TWO SIZES 2/9 AND 3/11